Praise for *My Divine Natural Hair*

"I can totally relate to many of the stories shared in *My Divine Natural Hair*. I am a naturalista (after trying three times to give up the relaxers I used for twenty-five years), and I am raising a teen daughter who has not had any chemicals touch her natural hair. I believe it's important for African American women to get in touch with our tresses. Knowing our hair correlates to knowing ourselves and truly loving who God has created us to be!"

—**Katara Washington Patton**, executive editor,
Our Daily Bread Ministries, and author of *Inspiration
for Christian Teen Girls* and *Navigating the Blues*

"Overall, *My Divine Natural Hair* is an empowering and informative read that goes beyond hair care tips. It delves into the emotional and cultural significance of natural Afro hair, providing valuable insights that inspire women to embrace their true selves, celebrate their unique beauty, and cultivate a loving relationship with their hair and identity. I highly recommend this book to women of all ages and backgrounds, as it offers a wealth of knowledge and encouragement for those on a journey of self-discovery and self-acceptance. I am excited about my natural hair journey in a fresh new way!"

—**Kamia White**, educator-podcaster, Beauty in Bloom, LLC

"This is the unique story of a unique family, about a unique topic: black women's hair. By artfully telling their black hair story, the trio of Burlock women have done a great service because their story is steeped in African American culture and is the personal story of most African American females."

—**Dr. Willie O. Peterson**, adjunct professor,
Dallas Theological Seminary; former trustee,
Denver Seminary Board; assistant to the superintendent,
Midsouth Conference, Evangelical Covenant Church

"This book is an adventure into 'us' that many African American women have been through and continue to grow through. Thank you for taking us step-by-step with such a real voice through where we are, have been, and continue to go. Thank you for opening our eyes in such an astute way to love what God gave us."

—**Clarissa W. Felder**, MS, MSBS, 1st Anti-Basileus
Phi Delta Kappa, National Sorority Inc., Beta Lambda

"*My Divine Natural Hair* is a must-read because of the personal and compelling stories of the hair journeys of the threesome, their struggles and victories, and the whys and hows of black hair. Beautifully written with love, candor, compassion, and hope, it encourages every black girl and woman to embrace her natural hair as God's testimony that she is 'fearfully and wonderfully made.'"

—**Prisca Onwuemene**, librarian (retired),
Winston-Salem (North Carolina)/Forsyth County Schools

"ASE! ASE! Giving thanks and praise for this soul-nourishing book. I thank the authors for this celebration of our natural beauty that the Creator has bestowed upon us—our crowns! I resonated with their stories, as I too felt I had to bow to the pressure to embrace society's standard of beauty. My decision to lock my hair (I've been locked since 2015) was a spiritual and healing journey to reclaim the essence of who I was meant to be as an expression of the Most High. This book will be so beneficial for those wanting to start on their own path to healing and self-acceptance."

—**Rebecca Wells Lewis**, RN Case Manager,
Certified Kemetic Yoga Teacher

"I have been so blessed to see 'my people' appreciate the way God has created us! This is what the authors of *My Divine Natural Hair* are communicating to us."

—**Norma Corley**, counselor, Winston-Salem
(North Carolina)/Forsyth County Schools

MY DIVINE
Natural Hair

INSPIRATION & TIPS TO LOVE & CARE FOR YOUR CROWN

SHELIA BURLOCK, SYLVIA BURLOCK & MELISSA BURLOCK

Broadleaf Books
Minneapolis

MY DIVINE NATURAL HAIR
Inspiration & Tips to Love & Care for Your Crown

The information and other content provided in this book, or in any provided materials,
are not intended and should not be construed as medical advice, nor is the information
a substitute for professional medical expertise or treatment. Consult with your health
care provider or seek other professional medical treatment. Never disregard professional
medical advice or delay in seeking it because of something that you have read in this
book. If you think you may have a medical emergency, call your doctor or emergency
services immediately.

Library of Congress Cataloging-in-Publication Data

Names: Burlock, Shelia, author. | Burlock, Sylvia, author. | Burlock, Melissa Grace,
    author.
Title: My divine, natural hair : inspiration & tips to love & care for your crown / by
    Shelia Burlock, Sylvia Burlock & Melissa Burlock.
Description: Minneapolis : Broadleaf Books, [2024]
Identifiers: LCCN 2023022864 (print) | LCCN 2023022865 (ebook) | ISBN
    9781506494012 (hardback) | ISBN 9781506494029 (ebook)
Subjects: LCSH: Hairdressing of African Americans. | Hairdressing of African
    Americans--Religious aspects--Christianity. | Hair--Care and hygiene. | African
    American women--Race identity. | African American women--Religious life.
Classification: LCC TT972 .B87 2024 (print) | LCC TT972 (ebook) | DDC
    646.7/2408996073--dc23/eng/20230905
LC record available at https://lccn.loc.gov/2023022864
LC ebook record available at https://lccn.loc.gov/2023022865

Cover design: 1517 Media
Cover illustrations by Nzilani Simu

Print ISBN: 978-1-5064-9401-2
eBook ISBN: 978-1-5064-9402-9

Printed in China.

CONTENTS

Salon Chair Sessions

INTRODUCTION

In Chad, the women say God left a gift in the mountains to make their hair grow.[1] If the flowering plant that produces the seeds, which these women have been blending into a silky powder and applying to their hair with oils for a millennium, is a gift from God, it would only be one of the innumerable ways the Creator's abundant grace is revealed through black women's crowns of glory.

There are crowns you see from afar on the heads of monarchs, and there are crowns you're born with. We wrote *My Divine Natural Hair: Inspiration & Tips to Love & Care for Your Crown* because our hearts are for black women to intimately know God's love for them and to embrace their natural hair—their physical crowns—as a gift from God. Regardless of hairstyle and especially in the wake of hair damage and hair loss, we wanted to take the spiritual crown of God's Word and place it squarely on your head, dear reader, then talk shop with you. That's why our book isn't about how to achieve the perfect hairdo; it's about how God, who numbers the very hairs on our heads (Luke 12:7 NLT), wants us to accept and love our natural coils and curls.

How to Approach Reading

Before beginning your reading journey through this book, pray. Pray for eyes to see your hair as God's indulgence, not a chore. Pray that your natural hair journey will be a spiritual journey as well. Pray for God to make plain how you can apply these readings both to *your thoughts toward your hair* and *your daily hair care regimen*. The stories and reflections in this book will apply to both.

My Divine Natural Hair is divided into three sections:

Hairmeneutics

Fittingly at the beginning of this book, this section is about how the book began: with our personal hair stories. Melissa shares her experience with hair loss as an adult and how this both hurt and ultimately led to the healing of her self-esteem. Sylvia talks about why she decided to start wearing her natural hair in high school and the challenges and opportunities she has encountered because of that decision. And Shelia reflects on the connection between how her mother did her hair as a child to the different styles she experimented with as an adult to how she styled Melissa's and Sylvia's hair when they were growing up. Like three strands of a braid, these stories form one intergenerational narrative about the black women in one family and their relationship to their natural hair, both individually and within a Bible-believing community. This section ends with contextualizing our stories within the history of historical hair trauma and the present-day natural hair community.

Reflections to Find the Divine in My Natural Hair

These fifty-two inspirational readings (around one to two pages each) are based on our personal experiences, principles from scripture, as well as popular culture. We stop at meaningful spaces that have become signposts along each of our natural hair journeys, from kitchen stove tops to salons, worship spaces to workplaces, hospital rooms to classrooms to bathroom mirrors. Each reading begins with a quote and/or scripture and concludes with an affirmation or a "hair prayer" about natural hair to help you meaningfully incorporate what you read into your day-to-day life. Recite the affirmations to encourage yourself in the morning or evening. Use these words as a prompt for a journal entry or devotional thought. Pray them as you speak to God specifically about your feelings toward your natural hair and invite your Creator into the intimacy of your decision-making process about beauty regimens, asking for both the desire and discipline to care for your hair.

Salon Chair Sessions

Just as the personal hair stories, inspirational readings, and spiritual reflections in the first and second sections of this book help you discover the divine beauty in your natural hair, this third section coaches you through your hair's ups and downs. Filled with practical tips for physically caring for your hair along with a healthy dose of encouragement, these forty-eight readings (each one is around three pages) will guide you throughout your natural hair journey, from bad hair days to picture-perfect moments. We begin with a long overdue discussion about hair textures and the problem with conventional hair type charts. Each reading after that covers a specific subject, like healthy hair care regimens, scalp health, DIY hair care recipes with essential oils, remedies for inflammation, as well as strategies for a host of hair-related issues, from how to detangle your hair to how to interpret ingredients on hair products. There is also a glossary of natural hair terminology used throughout the book at the end of this section.

Let Your Hair Up

We recommend reading Hairmeneutics first before moving on to Reflections and Salon Chair Sessions. Because the latter two sections are made up of shorter daily readings, feel free to read them in whatever order you would like, whether that is in the order they're printed, or based on the title and what kind of encouragement you feel you need that day. The Salon Chair Sessions especially are like a toolkit of detailed advice and information about your hair, so you can also use this section and the glossary as reference tools.

As you read, think of sitting in that kitchen chair next to the stove where the hot comb used to heat up generations ago, but now, instead, styling your natural hair. Get comfortable and let's chat.

HAIRMENEUTICS

Hermeneutics[1]

/hər-mə-ˈnü-tiks/ *noun*
1 the study of the methodological principles of interpretation (as of the Bible).
2 a method or principle of interpretation.

Hairmeneutics

/her-mə-ˈnü-tiks/ *noun*
1 the method of Biblical interpretation that reclaims black people's hair from a historical context of shame for the manifest glory God originally intended for Afro-textured hair.
2 the principle that God created kinky hair.

God even knows how many hairs are on your head.

—*Matthew 10:30 NCV*

MELISSA'S HAIR STORY: TRESSES & STRESSES

My mom, Shelia, my sister, Sylvia, and I (Melissa) wrote this book because of my hair story. Like so many black girls, when I think about the beginning of my hair story, I think of my mom sitting with me. Like she did on the couch while she braided my hair, or in the kitchen while the hot comb heated up on the stovetop, and then again, years later, on a hard plastic chair in a doctor's office.

"*What a beautiful turban*," the dermatologist had said as I disarmed myself of my black-and-white checkered headscarf and relinquished the fabric shield to my mom's hands.

"Thank you. It's a scarf."

"*Are you losing hair on any other part of your body?*"

"No."

"*What about your eyebrows?*"

"No, only on my scalp. In the crown."

My hair used to stand up from my head as if it had something important to say. The only direction it knew how to grow was up. Unhindered and unbound; unashamed, unafraid. My hair had once been a diadem of un-Rapunzel-like black coils that wrestled the weight of gravity every day, and won. I'd boast a braid that pointed straight up from the top of my head, like a strong tower reaching to the sky, and even beyond that visible firmament. Heavenward.

Mom knew, even before I was born, I was going to have a lot of hair. She once told me she experienced heartburn when she was pregnant with me and that her discomfort was a sign that I was going to have thick hair. My baby 'Fros and vertical-coiling braids proved that deduction true. Growing up, my sister and I played with black dolls and read children's books that featured black girls as main characters.

I remember sporting fat braids that ended in candy-colored snap barrettes and perfectly coiffed bangs that framed my face in elementary school. Our parents didn't allow my sister and me to get relaxers because Mom had experienced a chemical burn from a salon relaxer as a young woman. (She still has a tiny thin spot in the front of her hair to this day from a relaxer that wasn't rinsed out properly years ago.) So even though chemicals would have made my and my sister's hair straighter quicker (and for a longer period of time), Mom chose the hot comb to straighten our hair. She wanted our hair to be pretty, and for Mom, like her Madear before her, pretty hair meant straight hair. Two chairs by the kitchen stove became our first salon. Mom's hot comb would rest in the cool lair of a kitchen drawer until she drew it out and placed it on a medium-hot, orange-red eye of the electric stove. The searing hot comb hissed close to my skin and licked my hair straight with a pink-lotion-sweet, acrid sizzle as wisps of smoke swirled from its cast-iron teeth.

My sister, Sylvia, has a hair texture that bounces when touched; mine your hand sinks into. Our textures determined how long it took Mom to press our hair and how long the press lasted. My hair was thick, the coils indistinguishable from each other and inextricably enmeshed. My hair took longer to press straight, but hours after Mom's hot comb ironed the kinks out, mine dutifully held the shapes of the rollers without a frizz. Sylvia's hair didn't take as long to press, but a short while later, her pressed bangs playfully puffed back like a rain cloud ready to burst and extinguish the futile fire-heat of Mom's hot comb. I don't recall her minding that though. I, on the other hand, liked that my hair held a press. I liked how the heat unlocked secret inches of length hidden within the whorls of my tightly coiled hair strands. I had to have liked not sitting beside the stove as often. And I must have liked having hair like my mom's soft-pressed, red-brown curls.

I distinctly remember my and my sister's beaded hairstyles in middle school; they made me feel like we were Venus and Serena. My mom would braid our hair, then slide pea-sized beads onto each plait, one by one, with the dexterity of a mathematician counting figures on an abacus. Beads that made my hair a headful of "whippable" unclasped necklaces. I delighted in swooshing my beaded tendrils back and forth in a chime of clacks despite the fact that any quick movement would make the beads snap against my cheek with the force of an angry finger pop. My beads told the world I was cared for, that Mom spent hours doing my sister's and my hair. Each plastic piece a currency in the bank of my self-esteem.

"A relaxer isn't the same thing as a perm."

The year before Sylvia started middle school, I had my first day of high school. (We're four years apart.) It was then that our hairstyles diverged. I didn't want to wear the same hairstyles as my little sister anymore. I wanted to be "myself." In an ironic twist, that meant wearing the same types of straight hairstyles that most of the other black girls in my school wore. My parents still didn't want or pay for me to get my hair chemically straightened though (nor Sylvia), which was why they were pretty upset when I did just that.

My dad had dropped me off at a salon to get my hair "done," straightened with heat (not chemicals). The salon was recommended by a family friend who had promised that this particular hairstylist could do wonders or at least could magically transform my hair into a style that was more chic and mature than what Mom could do next to the kitchen stove with the wave of the old hot comb. *Maybe he would press it real fine and shape it into an updo . . . or maybe he would press it so good, it would stay straight and hang long for a week or longer, like how my auntie's hair did after years of pressing her hair.* I was surprised when, once it was my turn to sit in the salon chair, the hairstylist wanted to relax my hair. I told him I wasn't allowed to get a perm. He said that a relaxer wasn't the same thing as a perm. And after a few more words of friendly advice and soft persuasion, and because I kind of wanted to anyway, I agreed he was right. He relaxed my hair, and when I got back home, my parents were mad. I knew they were angry with the hairstylist and not with me though. And I got what I wanted: straight hair. Unlike the most expertly pressed hair, which stayed frozen in a style, my relaxed hair swished back and forth like water, "free" from the zig-zag bars of kinky coils.

Relaxing my hair didn't mean I thought that my natural hair was bad. To me, at the time, it meant that my hair was "done." (The only girls I knew who came out of their house wearing their natural hair, as their hair, without doing anything to it, were white.) I've been getting my hair "done" since I was a little girl sitting between Mom's knees while she braided my own hair. As I got older though, I aged out of those natural hairstyles with the cute barrettes and the beads. By the time I got to high school, getting my hair done meant changing my natural hair texture or getting braids (more on that later), like it seemed what everyone else around me was doing, if I wanted to fit in. Like most teenagers, I was self-conscious about fitting in with my peers. And as a black girl attending a majority-white public school, that meant fitting in within an environment where popular girls were either blonde or brunette or black girls who straightened their hair. Though I didn't think it was bad, my hair wasn't the standard in that context. Trying to fit in was especially important to me because I was already shy and socially awkward; I didn't want my hair to also stand out (i.e., stand up) as different.

Besides wanting to straighten my hair, I think that hairstylist was also able to easily convince me that "relaxing wasn't the same as perming," and basically to disobey what my parents told me not to do because I was curious. I wanted to know what chemically straightened hair would look like on me because I'd never experienced it before. After I got my hair relaxed for the first time though, the newness of the experience soon wore off. My hair was straight, but I noticed it was thin. My relaxed tendrils didn't "flow" as freely as they did after I'd first gotten it done, and all I could eventually do was rubberband them into a short ponytail at the nape of my neck. My hair was straight, but it was also flat.

I didn't continue to go to the hairstylist who'd put the relaxer in my hair. I ended up growing out that relaxer. Still, I don't think I regretted getting one. Because of it, I had crossed a line into a realm where straightening my natural hair wasn't a disallowed impossibility.

Princess of S-Curls

The Jheri curl sounded old-fashioned to me when I was in high school, maybe because my cultural references for the hairstyle were Michael Jackson in the music video for "Thriller" and that Soul Glo commercial in the film *Coming to America*. I didn't know anyone else who was wearing a Jheri curl, and I couldn't imagine how I would look if I did. If Mom hadn't suggested it as an alternative to getting my hair relaxed again, I wouldn't have thought to try.

I think Mom's thinking was that if I wanted to chemically straighten my hair, I should use the same products that, unlike the salon and box perms, hadn't broken off her hair. She said that the Jheri curl had actually made her hair grow when she wore the style in the '80s. Disillusioned with the effects of the relaxer, and hoping I could have straightened hair that didn't look thin, I asked her to put the Jheri curl in my hair. I remember those rainbow-colored perm rods had the same painful snap as my beads used to when they came out, leaving behind, to my pure delight, a head full of soft ebony S-curls. Mom had been right; I adored my new style. The Jheri curl loosened my fist-tight corkscrew natural coils into defined spirals without compromising the thickness of my hair and even seemed to make my hair grow longer. It made me feel like my hair was *me*, only enhanced because it wasn't flattened beyond resemblance like when I had a relaxer. It made me feel "my age," mature, because I was wearing my hair differently than how I did growing up. Maintaining it was a chore though.

I remember hurriedly spritzing my thirsty curls with activator spray in the restroom in between classes. While my hairdo was never quite drenched enough to leave a dark, head-shaped stain on a high-back couch, there were the inevitable stains on my shirt and jacket collars. I came to realize why Mom had stopped wearing the style even though it had made her hair grow at the time: it took time and attention, usually multiple times a day, to keep up. I grew out the Jheri curl and went to a beautician (different from the one who put in the relaxer) to get a relaxer for my junior prom, which my parents were okay with since it was a special occasion. Being styled in a pretty updo for prom was great, but during my day-to-day, the relaxer made my hair straight and flat. By the time I was a senior, I decided to give myself a break from the task of maintaining chemically straightened hairstyles and switched to the perennially popular hairstyle for black girls: braids.

Asian Beauty Stores & African Hair Braiding Salons

The braids I wore in high school were not the childhood ones Mom had created. Barrettes and beads were replaced by bundles of silky synthetic hair as necessary accoutrements. The added hair was to make my braids longer and thicker than they would be without it. To obtain the added hair, I couldn't go to a Sally's, Target, or another store that carried basic hair care supplies. I went to the proverbial beauty supply store.

They were always located near downtown or in older parts of the city, outside of the typical radius of where I lived in the suburbs, and predominantly owned by Korean Americans.[1] And they were primarily patronized by African-American women about to get their hair done, like me. Going through the doors of one of these stores the first couple of times was like entering a new world. I would navigate aisles overflowing with a wonderland of weaves and wigs of every shade, length, and cut beneath clusters of ceiling-mounted security monitors that tracked my movements across unblinking screens. I'd buy my color amid the wall display of plastic-sheathed hair bundles: #1B. Ebony black. Sometimes when I was there, I also got Mom hers: #2. Reddish-brown.

My mom had been getting her hair braided by a hairstylist who would come over to our house. My sister and I called her Ms. P. She started braiding my and my sister's hair too. Together, me and her would sit in the living room and talk for hours as the bundles of hair shrank and my shoulder-length braids increased one by one, each one slighter than the width of a pencil. Tough but soft-spoken, petite and not much taller than I was in high school, she'd tell my sister and me hilarious stories.

The main style Ms. P did for me was cornrows in the front, braids in the back. When she was done, she'd use a neon pink lighter to melt the tips of the braids together to keep them from unraveling, the last step in an hours-long process that she spent all on her feet while I sat in a kitchen folding chair. I also remember twisting my finished braids around perm rods, dipping them in a chipped mug of steaming hot water, and then toweling them off. Once the rods were removed, the ends of the braids would be shaped like bouncy springs. Ms. P became family, one of my aunties. She and her husband came to Mom's graduation from her master's program and to church with our family, and I hung out over at their house. Other than Mom, Ms. P was the woman who had her fingers in my hair the most. That would be the last time I had a personal relationship with the person who braided my hair. After I graduated and relocated to another state for college, getting my hair done became less relational, more transactional.

In college, I shifted from sometimes wearing braids to only wearing braids, for convenience. No daily activator spritzes for a Jheri curl in between rushing to classes on campus. No experimenting with other ways to straighten or style my hair when I needed to spend hours studying for exams, writing research papers, and memorizing presentations. Me and my hair saw each other every month or so, when I washed and picked out my thick mass of coarse hair, tied and stuffed it underneath a hat, and went to a hair braiding salon, anticipating that the bundles of hair in my hand would become braids on my head by the time I left.

The African hair braiding salons were not far from the beauty supply stores. Going into one of these salons, I would sometimes need to wait for an open chair, regardless if I had called ahead and made an "appointment." Walk-ins were welcomed, and it was first come, first served. When a hairstylist was free, I would give her my packs of synthetic hair, slide into a swivel salon chair, and brace myself against the initial daggered twist of pain as the hairstylist anchored some of the added hair to my scalp and started braiding it with my own natural hair into the first long, perfect braid. One down. Hundreds more to go.

I don't remember passing the time reading, and this would have been before smartphones. Just being in that chair for six to eight hours, in that space, where the Senegalese hairstylists were chatting in French to each other over the sound of a Nollywood film on the staticky TV monitor, was enough. I was one of many heads in various stages of completion, which you could tell by how much of a woman's natural hair was out in short tufts versus how much of it was in braids down her back. The hair braiding salon was a space where we were safe to let our hair up, remove our ball caps or scarves to reveal a part of ourselves that the majority of us covered up every other day of the week with one style or another.

Otherwise a tale of two worlds, the Asian beauty supply store and the African hair braiding salon were the same in that they were both spaces that existed for me as a black woman. I bought my hair. I got my hair braided. I didn't have to put up with hearing anyone ask, "But that's not your *real* hair?" or having someone gasp about the amount of time it took to braid my hair. I was the majority in these spaces. There was no shame. At the hair braiding salon especially, I and every other black woman, whether first-generation African immigrants or

African Americans, were all gathered there in the name of getting our hair done.

"It looks real."

It didn't happen all at once, my edges starting to thin. By the time I was a senior in college, the breakage around my temples had resulted in a less-than-full hairline due to not building in breaks between taking my braids down and getting them reinstalled. Even though braided hairstyles with added hair can help with hair growth, they can also lead to breakage if worn too long and too often without giving the hair time to rest (see Salon Chair Session 4S "Damaging Styling Practices"). It wasn't only my edges though. I remember thinking that all of my hair was in bad shape and just not happy. The tension that came from constantly getting tight braid styles damaged my hair and my scalp, causing uneven breakage and inflammation.

Also, washing my hair had become a chore. Because I knew that I was getting my hair braided with added hair soon and not wearing it on its own in any particular style, my habit was to rush through the hair care process. I didn't follow a multi-step regimen to replenish my hair's nutrients or soften its dryness before or after washing. For me, wash day was a necessary obstacle, one to get through as efficiently as I could to get my hair ready to be braided, which was usually within a few days of taking it down. I remember one instance when I was particularly rough with picking my hair. Even though my hair wasn't its healthiest, it still was a lot. It rose up toward the ceiling of the restroom, a dense dark profusion that I was lost as to what to do with except rake with mounting frustration. I attacked my coils like they were enemies, wielding my wide-tooth comb in an effort to slay the multiplying fairy knots and stubborn tangles. *Why couldn't I just comb it? Run my fingers through it like I could with the silky synthetic hair I bought from the beauty supply store?*

I couldn't keep going back to the hair braiding salon because of the damage caused by back-to-back braid styles. Neither did I want to risk straightening my hair with harsh chemicals or experimenting with a tight sew-in weave in its current state. I decided it would be best to switch to wearing a wig. I went to the beauty supply store again, but this time, instead of looking for packs of synthetic hair, I browsed a section at the back of the store I had up until then ignored. Styrofoam heads stood on top and inside of glass counters and on floor-to-ceiling shelves covering the back walls, all of them sporting a different style of straight-hair wig. There were wigs with short bob pixie cuts, asymmetrical cuts, wigs with twenty-inch-long densely wavy curls, wigs with curtain bangs, wigs with hot pink roots, wigs with honey-brown or aquamarine blue highlights, salt-and-pepper wigs, cropped curly wigs, and the ultra-glamorous 100 percent virgin hair (or human hair) wigs locked inside of glass display cases, no doubt waiting for their chance in the limelight on the heads of Beyoncé's backup singers. It was overwhelming because I hadn't had that much experience with wigs. There was the short reddish-brown one my mom wore years before that; Sylvia had once borrowed it when she dressed up as Madame C. J. Walker for a class project in elementary school. There was the "church" wig my grandma wore on Sundays. I didn't know the pros and cons of synthetic hair versus human hair wigs (except that the latter were alarmingly expensive to a college student on a limited budget) nor had I ever heard of lace-front, full lace, lace part, undetectable invisible lace, glueless, pre-plucked, Brazilian, Peruvian, etc.

It took me a while to walk through the huge selection multiple times before deciding on one I wanted. I picked up the disembodied mannequin, paid the mandatory $1 at the counter to purchase a wig cap, pulled on my first lace-front unit, and studied my reflection in the wide mirror, turning my face from side to side. The synthetic hair felt weightless. The soft black hair was straight, but the ends curved inward like the bottom of a C to gently graze my shoulders. I had ignored the wigs that would have hung down past my shoulders in impossibly dense waves and others that, in my mind, would have made me look like I was wearing a wig to other people. I remember that I specifically wanted a wig that looked like what I imagined my own hair would naturally look like . . . if I had gotten a relaxer or a sew-in weave. I went to a historically black college and saw an array of beautiful black hairstyles on friends and peers: permed, locked, Afros, and braids. I was embarrassed to wear a wig to cover the damage to my natural hair. My thinking was that, if my wig looked "real," then it would disguise that embarrassment.

The first lace-front unit I tried on in the beauty store checked the "real" box. I repositioned the wig on the mannequin and handed it to the clerk, an Asian woman whose hair was as ebony and silky as the wig I had tried on. "I want this one," I said. The clerk disappeared through a storage door and soon returned with a shiny black rectangular box. I paid, miraculously, less than $100 for the new wig, walked briskly past the wall of synthetic hair bundles, and left the store. That lace-front unit became part of the uniform of "me" every day going to class and out on the weekends: shoes, jeans, top, earrings, and my lace-front unit. I watched YouTube tutorials to learn how to snip off the sheath of lace that extended from the front of the wig and I figured out how to use the combs in the front and back to snugly position it in place over the elastic-band wig cap covering my cornrows.

I knew I had made the perfect choice when I heard a fellow student talking about sew-ins and how the best ones looked "natural" (i.e., as if the extensions actually grew straight from the scalp) if the beautician knew what she was doing. I remembered this particular student wore caramel-colored curly braids. She happened to be walking past where I was sitting when she paused and unexpectedly bent down to peer at the hairline of my lace-front wig. I stiffened. She quickly straightened and, nodding affirmatively, pronounced, "It looks real." I exhaled in relief. Inside, I rejoiced.

The Devil Is a Lye & the Truth About Glue-In Tracks

By the time I moved back to my hometown to start grad school a year after college, my relationship with my hair was literally out of touch. We didn't see each other much, other than when my coils needed to be washed, picked out, and flat twisted before being covered by a wig cap and lace-front unit again.

I had gotten used to washing my unit in the bathtub and buying a new one when the lace of my old unit stopped fitting as snugly after multiple washes. I never matched the success of that first lace-front though; my succeeding wigs, though nice, never fit as perfectly as my first one and I had to try on several wigs in the beauty supply store before I made a purchase.

The health of my natural hair, though it had initially improved beneath a wig because of being able to rest from chemicals and tight braid extensions, had started to decline from not regularly coming out from beneath a wig. My coils became consistently dry, broken off a couple of inches in some places. And I was tired of always wearing wigs. I wanted to wear my own hair again in a mature style and, based on what I was used to, that meant going from wearing straight bob wigs back to straightening my own hair.

Before grad school, the last time a hairstylist had chemically straightened my natural hair was when I was a teenager. Getting my hair relaxed as an adult was different. My head was on fire. When the beautician finally doused my head under running water, rinsing off the creamy substance, I felt him stroke my thick tresses in the sink. Back in the salon chair, with my coils baptized by fire to emerge newly silky straight, the styling could begin. The beautician dried my freshly straightened hair. He trimmed my ends. He gave me a sleek pixie cut, the shortest I had ever worn my hair. Then, as if all of that was a prelude, he parted and glued hair extensions directly onto my own hair, layering the satiny black tracks close to the scalp, in the crown of my head. (The extensions were probably synthetic, not human hair, but I can only guess.) Although it is common to add extensions to chemically straightened hair to create a full, "lush" look, I hadn't asked the beautician to do this to my hair. I was only familiar with hair extensions that came in bundles to be braided, not attached with an adhesive. I was surprised, but I didn't say anything to stop the beautician. I trusted him. I remember being thankful to him for being nice to me and not making me feel judged about how dry and broken off my natural hair had been. I assured myself he was the expert. When he was done and I swiveled my salon chair around to look at my reflection, I wasn't thinking about losing my hair, bald spots, or any of the possible consequences of relaxers or weaves. I was imagining the compliments I'd receive from peers and even strangers. I anticipated how confident and attractive I would feel walking into a room. When

I went to class the next day and was greeted by exclamations about how beautiful and perfect the style was for me, I knew I had the right one.

After that first salon visit, I delegated the weekly stewardship of my hair to my beautician. Meanwhile, Sylvia told me over a Steak 'n Shake meal, "You shouldn't keep getting tracks glued onto your hair." I refused to stop going to this hairdresser though. It had become mundane for me to prioritize my appearance over my comfort and potential well-being. I never questioned my beautician about gluing the hair track directly on my relaxed hair, nor asked him to discontinue doing it, because I too liked the end result. I smiled at the extra *umph* at the front of my short style. I enjoyed the way the glossy hair hung sleek and thick as a raven's wing in a swoop across my forehead. In comparison, I didn't like my natural hair enough to show it like I did when I could wear pressed styles and beads in my childhood and preteens.

My natural hair was me. Straightened hair was me with a superhero cape. With straightened hair, I felt any outfit I wore was enhanced somehow. I felt that straight hair, whether wigs or extensions, transformed me into someone who met the visual standard of what society around me pedestalized as professional, mature, in style, and beautiful. Mainstream culture's standard for what texture of hair could be considered "good" had become my own.

Rather than raising the bar, this standard was actually a huge step down from what my sister and I learned growing up, playing with black dolls and adoring our beaded hairdos. What mattered to me as a young adult was feeling worthy of other people's praise, feeling beautiful to myself when I looked in a mirror and combed my fingers through the straight hair that I saw most black women sporting in my daily life and on

TV. The health of my scalp did not matter; it was not something I even seriously worried about.

After finishing grad school, I stopped getting my hair relaxed and styled with extensions at the salon. I needed to save money. I also needed to decide what I wanted to do with my degree. Relaxed hair cannot return to its former natural state, so while I looked for a 9-to-5, I started growing it out. My new growth (which was my natural hair texture) got longer and, eventually, I cut off the relaxed ends of my hair and had a short Afro. I wasn't going into an office with mostly white colleagues, so I was fine wearing my own hair as it grew out from my scalp because there wasn't any immediate day-to-day audience to look good for. My only audience was me in the mirror. It turned out I was tough to please. Sylvia, who was wearing her natural hair in twists by then (more on her hair story later), would look in the mirror beside me and try to convince me that I was beautiful wearing my Afro. Once, she'd even put a necklace around my neck, had me put on some lipstick, and said, "See?" pointing to my reflection. But I didn't see. I only saw where my hairline had thinned or receded. I saw short, uneven tufts of dense coils. I saw what I didn't love—my natural hair. I would never commit to wearing my hair in a TWA (teeny-weeny Afro) or another natural hairstyle indefinitely, especially when I had to start going to work every day in a professional environment.

By getting my fingers in my own hair for a while instead of going to the salon, I ascertained that the thinning spaces in my hair were now bald spots. The beautician had been hiding them with the glue-in tracks. Sylvia would take "state-of-Melissa's-hair" photos while I was seated or bending down, then show them to me so I could see the two dime-size clean spots perpendicular to each other in the crown of my head.

They began as twin oases amid a flaming bush of Afro hair that desperately wanted to reclaim its lost ground. Tracking the breakage in the crown area was the reason I eventually went with Mom to see a dermatologist.

On some days, I wore head scarves as an alternative to wearing my hair out. I'd worn scarves when I slept at night for as long as I could remember: black silk scarves underneath stocking caps; voluminous sleeping bonnets when I wore braids; wrap strips to hold my relaxed hair in place, etc. Like many black and brown girls, I never went to bed without wearing something on my head. For going out of the house though, I needed decorative head scarves—the long, colorfully patterned sort you could tie into buns and turbans. Sylvia, who at this point had been buying natural hair products from US-based, black-woman-owned beauty stores, bought me my first patterned headwrap from one of these online shops: a black-and-white checkered scarf made of soft, quality fabric. I bought more, usually in black or white because I felt those would be easier to match with anything I wore. Mom was the first to teach me the basics of how to tie a head wrap; she'd worn them a lot when she was in college. Soon I was able to quickly tie my head wraps in two go-to styles: a low bun in the back of my head and a braided crown in which I secured the scarf then twisted and wrapped the two "tails" around my head and tucked them in the back. I liked the look and ease of my head wraps, but I still didn't equate them with wearing straightened hair. I saw them as a casual option, not a professional style. I opted for the black-and-white checkered scarf that Sylvia gifted me when I went with Mom to the dermatologist because I could wrap it in a snug, braided crown style. The stiffness of the fabric meant that the wrap kept its circular shape on Mom's lap, which made it easier to slip it back on after the dermatologist and her assistant took a biopsy sample from my scalp.

By this time, the hair around my bald spots had increasingly thinned. A few days later, the dermatologist, a white woman with a kind, European-accented voice, phoned to tell me, "You have central centrifugal cicatricial alopecia." What the dermatologist didn't know to tell me, and what I later found out through my own research, was that CCCA is a form of hair loss that is commonly experienced by black women. While previously believed to be solely attributable to the tight hairstyles and harsh chemicals we use on our hair at early ages, current research suggests that CCCA can be linked to multiple factors including genetics. CCCA destroys hair follicles and this leads to inflammation, scarring (cicatricial), and permanent hair loss, more often than not starting in the central part of the scalp or the crown.[2]

Hairstyles & Hiding Spaces

I was confident I could reverse the CCCA. At that time, I still had a lot of my coarse, tightly coiled natural hair, enough that the bald spots were invisible when I gathered my coils into a small Afro puff on the top of my head. The dermatologist even said she knew of another patient who completely reversed her hair loss after a similar diagnosis. Buoyed by this account and the doctor's recommendations to use men's Rogaine to treat my current hair loss around my edges, I didn't sink into despair. There was hope to stimulate hair growth.

I went to CVS, to an aisle I'd never been to before in my life, and bought men's Rogaine. I started applying it topically to my edges, keeping Mom posted about the fuzzy new growth that emerged. Mom went with me to a clinic that specialized in using blue light treatments to regrow hair, which I ultimately didn't feel comfortable enough about to pursue. I believed I could stimulate my hair growth naturally from the inside out, but first, I had to treat my scalp.

Sylvia had started her beauty care blog and 100-percent-natural lipstick line, Beautifēk, by then, and she began focusing her research on different essential oil mixes and hair care recipes I could use to heal my scalp inflammation. She taught me the cleansing washes and the natural humectants that soothed and ultimately cured the inflamed bumps and sores that broke out on my scalp (see Salon Chair Sessions 5S "Hair Cleansers, Cleansing Washes" and 34S "Honey, Humectants & Humidity"). Once my scalp healed, I began regularly massaging essential oils into the bald spots and surrounding areas as well as started taking biotin.

Perhaps I could have reversed or at least prevented future hair loss had I made up my mind to continue wearing my natural hair while nurturing its weak areas. When I got my first salaried job though, my mindset shifted from healing the damage done to my hair and scalp to covering it up. Weighing the health of my hair against its acceptability or assimilability had become a survival mechanism for me, as it is for many other black women in the workplace today. A 2023 CROWN Workplace Research Study commissioned by Dove and LinkedIn found that black women who wear their natural coily/Afro-textured hair in the workplace are two times as likely to be the target of microaggressions than black women with straightened hair, and that "black women's hair is 2.5x more likely to be perceived as unprofessional."[3] Moreover, according to a previous CROWN Research Study conducted by JOY Collective in 2019, 80 percent of black women are more likely than women of other ethnicities to change the appearance of their natural hair in order to meet societal expectations and social norms in the workplace.[4] As black women, we choose between wearing our natural hair and experiencing hair discrimination in majority-white spaces and altering its texture to meet mainstream societal standards of what is "good," i.e., professional, beautiful, and compliment-worthy hair. We choose to either represent, or conform. At the time, I conformed.

I began working in an office where I was one of two black people. Most of my coworkers were white women with straight hair. Lace-front human hair wigs became my fig leaf of choice. When I would tire of wearing a lace-front unit and wanted to give my scalp some air on a day-to-day basis, I cornrowed my hair with added synthetic hair. The kind of hair I used was textured, unlike the straight hair I bought for my appointments at African braiding salons. I installed the braids myself in a fraction of the time it would take to get my hair braided. Rather than helping my scalp though, the cornrows sometimes caused inflammation. When I first showed Sylvia my flare-ups and sores, she'd helped me treat the inflammation with a natural hair care recipe that contained raw honey and said I should stop wearing tight cornrows. I didn't listen. I liked how thick the added hair made my cornrows look. I reasoned that the style wouldn't damage my hair because I didn't braid my hair all the time; it was only when I wanted to come out from underneath the wigs for a while.

I also began to combine the textured hair with my own hair, which was still long and thick around the balding spots in the crown, to create shoulder-length twists that were thick enough for me to expertly, I thought, cover the bald spots on my scalp. I would pull the twists to the side of my head with the weakest hairline to hide the edges. I would pull the braids toward the back of my head to hide the thinning spaces there. I watched YouTube tutorials on how to make the added textured hair look seamless with my own natural hair and collected an assortment of rubber bands, headbands, hair ties, and bobby pins to arrange and style my twists to the extent that my bathroom cupboard looked like a shelf in the beauty aisle at Target. Wearing twists was a compromise with my natural hair: I could wear my natural hair out, but just make it longer and thicker with the added textured hair. I could allow my scalp to breathe, but hide its balding areas and hair breakage. I could continue to use essential oil massages and hair care recipes for any flare-ups at night, but still wear a hairstyle with straight hair during the day.

One weekend, when my friend and I were walking around a packed convention center in downtown Indianapolis at the Black Expo, weaving our way through bodies and booths with countless health products on display, I felt a tap on my shoulder. I turned around and an older black woman, probably in her late sixties, peered up at me. Apparently, she'd decided to follow me to ask if I was using a hair regrowth product advertised at one of the booths. I looked like I needed it for the back of my head, she explained. I politely replied that I wasn't associated with that seller and she apologized, embarrassment shading her eyes. As we parted, I was burning inside. A week or so before, I'd twisted my hair back in thick cornrows with added hair and made a bun at the nape of my neck. I had been careful to cover the thin spots underneath the cornrows by pulling and twisting my hair around them, but the spaces in between the cornrows had widened since the last time I did the style. I thought it wasn't noticeable—until that encounter. I spent the rest of the Expo waiting to get back home to take out that hairstyle. The next day, I wore a wig, and the day after that, and the day after that. I didn't wear my natural hair out again, added hair or otherwise.

Wigs again became my go-to. I can scroll through photos of vacations and birthdays and outings over the years and tell you the kind of wig I had on in every single one: a straight bob wig, a wig styled in an over-the-shoulder fishtail braid, a wig tied in a low bun. All of them black and always straight.

I wasn't comfortable with shaving my head completely bald. I still somehow hoped my hair would grow back and promised myself that when it did, I'd be confident enough to wear it out again like I did when I wore braids in high school and college or TWAs after graduate school. The straight hair wigs I donned in the meantime compensated for what I felt I lacked in comparison with women who dressed better, spoke better, did their makeup better than me, and had naturally straight or straightened hair. I didn't want people to see the broken me with CCCA. I wanted people to see the "me" with straight, healthy hair. Straight hair conjured up *the* image of beauty for me. As black women, we fall under the same spell when we heap praises at the feet of a biracial celebrity with ultra-sleek straight hair or run adoring fingers through our own freshly relaxed hair on an Instagram live. Straight hair is glamorous. Straight hair magically sets our hair "free" by arresting our corkscrew-tight coils and locking them in line. For me at this point in my life, straight hair wigs shielded the hair breakage and bald spots caused by my CCCA and made my hair, and by extension me, beautiful.

I thought it would be easy to keep up my post-alopecia diagnosis regimens—to moisturize my own hair and massage my scalp every evening—if I could just stuff my skinny twists or tiny Bantu knots underneath wig caps and then underneath wigs. But, after working, commuting, stopping by the store, making dinner, taking out the trash, doing the dishes, and last-minute laundry, when I finally sat down on the couch for the first time all day for an hour before needing to go to bed, to do it all over again, my hair became a last priority. I was too tired to moisturize my parched hair or massage essential oils into the widening bald spots on my scalp. I wore a wig at work five days a week. I wore a wig when I went out after work. I wore a wig when I ran errands on Saturdays and when I attended church on Sundays. Why spend time moisturizing my hair when I wasn't actually wearing it? When I was stuffing it beneath a lace-front unit?

I grew weary of caring for my natural hair beneath the wigs. I became less and less consistent, less and less self-disciplined. In this season of negligence, the alopecia spread across the crown of my head. I didn't look in the mirror much anymore except with a wig on. When I did, my hair looked: *Bald. Broken. Ugly. Sickly. Humiliating.*

The little girl who'd boast a braid like a tower pointing straight up from the top of her head toward heaven and beyond was now an adult living with the broken ruins of that tower hidden beneath a new wig from the beauty supply store.

Mirror Reflections

During the coronavirus pandemic, when I wasn't going into the office, I began cutting my hair. I still had a hairline and edges, though the edges on the right side of my face (close to where the beautician laid the glue-in tracks) were significantly thinner than those on the left side. As typical with female pattern baldness, my hair loss and thinness were concentrated on the top of my head, as well as in the crown.[5] My hair on the back of my head was still so thick that caring for it took me hours to pre-poo, wash, condition, twist, and then moisturize. Worst, allowing the sections of hair I did have to grow along my hairline, edges, and in the back of my head made the widening bald spots in the crown of my head look balder. I imagined I resembled that character in *The Three Stooges*, the one with bunches of hair on the right and left sides of his head who lifted his hat to reveal—surprise!—no hair up top. It felt laughable. So, I cut the hair that I had as close as I could to my scalp with a pair of hair-cutting scissors.

After wearing a wig during the day for virtual meetings, I'd switch to scarves after logging off. I couldn't endure wearing nothing on my head around the house, lest I glimpse my reflection in the mirror above the bathroom sink or the accent mirror in the dining room or some other glassy surface and it silently scream at me. *Bald. Broken. Ugly. Sickly. Humiliating.* I'd fret with overanxious thoughts like: *What if I need to run out of the house for an emergency? Do I have a beanie nearby? Where's my ball cap? What if I were rushed to the emergency room and the nurses took off my scarf?*

I considered undergoing treatments like hair transplantation, which is a surgical procedure that involves moving healthy hair follicles to bald or balding areas of the scalp, or just shaving off all my hair. But I wasn't comfortable or confident enough to make either choice. Instead, I daydreamed about the thinning and bald spots of my hair miraculously growing back even though I'd given up on even taking care of the hair I had left. My wig-wearing routine had become a rut. Beneath all the 1B human and synthetic hair and occasional head wraps, I was stuck. Hiding. Hiding my alopecia underneath wigs and away from other people's eyes—even my own.

I'd only cut my hair a few times when my sister found out. I didn't announce when I did it; I waited until sections of my hair grew a few inches, snipped-snipped-snipped them down to barely a centimeter, tied up the evidence in a grocery store bag, pitched it, and kept wearing wigs and scarves. Sylvia finally realized what I'd been doing when I walked out of my bedroom, forgetting to cover my hair for a second, and she saw all my hair cut off. Besides dermatologists, my sister and my mom were the only ones who saw me without a wig or scarf. They cared more about my own hair than I did. After I told Mom that I was periodically cutting my hair (since Sylvia already knew), she and Sylvia together convinced me to grow my hair out where it could grow. After years of shrugging off their advice about what to do/not to do with my hair, I finally took it. The deal was I'd grow out the parts of my hair that I could, and once it was long enough, Mom would do cornrows—not too tight—without any added hair. If there was no growth, I'd shave it.

That first time Mom cornrowed my new growth, I remember my scalp was very tender. It was as if it'd forgotten what it was like to actually be touched or been angry at being awakened from a long hibernation. It took longer than it should have, not because of the amount of hair I had, but because Mom had to braid very lightly and slowly and then take out braids and rebraid if I said they felt too tight.

Two weeks later, I took the cornrows down and glanced in the mirror. What I saw made me stop and stare, shocked at my reflection. My hair, in the crown of my scalp, where it had begun to thin and bald, had actually grown back. Not a lot. But I could see traces of the evidence: Soft whorls sprouting here and there where it'd been barren mere weeks before. Mom's cornrows, the ones I hadn't worn since she used to braid my hair as a little girl, seemed to have stimulated my scalp.

Crowns

After those first signs of growth, I went back to practicing the hair care regimens I had learned right after I found out I had scarring alopecia. I massaged my scalp with a mixture of essential oils every evening (see Salon Chair Sessions 42S "Best Oils for Scalp Massage" and 27S "Embracing Those in Our Community Who Have Alopecia & Alopecia Remedies"). I highlighted "wash days" on my calendar and kept my appointments. I pre-pooed, shampooed, applied leave-in conditioner, oil, and cream products (in that order to complete the LOC Method for washing natural hair), and then sat on a floor pillow as Mom braided my hair in cornrows. I started using a goat hair brush, the kind for babies, to gently brush the weak spaces of my scalp and I felt this action further stimulated the parts that were not completely scarred over.

I started caring for my hair just to care for my hair, with no end result in mind, no plan to look good for other people. Meanwhile, Mom's cornrows grew thicker. My scalp became healthy and I was less tender-headed. The hair in my crown, while nowhere near full, started filling in, coil by coil. I still saw balding and brokenness. But when Mom and Sylvia looked at my hair, they excitedly proclaimed new growth. Where I had hopelessness, they had faith. What made me ashamed, made them proud.

Instead of covering my scalp's damage and alopecia with added hair and wigs, I was covered—in the Biblical sense— by the community of my mother and sister, encouraging and coaching me to honor my hair care regimens. I was covered by Mom's hair prayers over me. I was covered by my sister's affirmations of the beauty of my natural hair. Because of the words they spoke over me, words God has promised for me, I could trade the broken crown of my physical head for a spiritual crown of beauty and self-confidence, believing that my identity begins with how my God, the One who knows the number of coils on my head, sees me. What God put inside of me to reflect glory—my creativity, my spirit–matters more than what is (or isn't) on my head when I look at my reflection.

I wear an array of colorful head wraps now and occasionally don my favorite lace-front wig, but not because I'm ashamed of my hair texture or hair trauma any longer. I cover my natural hair for stylistic choice or protection, not because I think my hair is too time-consuming, ugly, or unmanageable. When I look in the mirror—CCCA notwithstanding—I can see how far I've come and I smile. And when I have enough hair to leave behind the head coverings and start photographing memories that aren't mileposted by different wigs, I'll smile too. Because my hair has a new story to tell about me now. *New. Blessed. Beautiful. Hopeful. Crowned.* Unhindered and unbound; unashamed, unafraid.

Maybe you think it's ironic for a book with natural hair in the title to be introduced by someone who has hair loss. Maybe you even judge me, because yes, I'm guilty. The form of hair loss I have isn't the kind men and women are diagnosed with from a young age. The extent of hair loss I've experienced is the consequence of placing the heaviest of burdens—the chemicals and hairstyles that I and many black women use to alter, "do," and hide our natural hair texture—on the fragilest of hair textures. The hair loss I've experienced is my fault.

Writing this book is covering myself with a new story instead of a wig. It is my way of accepting my alopecia. A way of forgiving myself. I forgave myself. Now I can grow—both myself and my hair. Hair care, after all, is spiritual care and self-care.

My own natural hair journey is a testament to this for it has been both a spiritual and physical journey toward grace.

I'm still on my natural hair journey. Mom and my sister walked alongside me even when I made the wrong choices, for the wrong reasons. They stood with me when I was healing. They are beside me now. It is our experience with my alopecia as a family that became the inspiration for this book.

Wherever you are on your natural hair journey, Mom, my sister, and I can tell you this: The One who created us crowned us first. Shining atop our heads is a divine diadem with all the lightness of air, radiance of honor, and the weight of glory. Whether or not our hair is growing, going, graying, or thinning from central centrifugal cicatricial alopecia or another form of hair loss, we wear an invisible crown bestowed on us by our Creator, that has always been there.

Along with the fractals in snowflakes, the curved petals of flowers, and everything else that has been created, our coils are wound around God's baby finger of eternity. And indeed, our coils are *very* good. As we practice accepting our God-given hair texture in a society that idolizes long and straight hair, let's remember that we don't just have hair stories. We have hair testimonies.

SYLVIA'S HAIR STORY: CLOSING THE DRAWER ON THE HOT COMB

When my sister and I (Sylvia, here) saw a hot comb on display in an exhibition, we laughed because, while at the museum it was being displayed as a relic, we knew too well how modern it felt to us. We need to allow the hot comb to stay where it belongs—in the past. And that old, forgotten hot comb in the drawer of my parents' kitchen? I'm metaphorically closing the drawer every time I choose to wear my natural hair. This is my hair story.

Getting my hair pressed was like trying to get every kink to lay down straight. The things we go through for our hair. Or rather, the things I've put myself through to try to conform my hair to "straight" beauty standards.

I remember only taking baths because a shower would "turn my hair back." All it took was some moisture and my pressed hair would be no more than a cloud of kinky hair. At school, between passing periods, I would rush off to the girls' restroom to brush or comb my hair, ensuring that it looked pristine. I even would ask my mom to take pictures of me with my pressed hair in front of our doorstep before leaving for school. I have more than one "photo shoot" I took of myself where I am wearing straight hair. Apparently, it was a thing in my early high school days.

But, by my senior year, something had changed. I can't quite put my finger on it. Maybe it was the fact my mom found a natural hairstylist who made my hair grow. Or maybe it was the fact I didn't care much about what other kids at school thought anymore. Or maybe it was one of the first times I genuinely began to love my hair for how it grew out of my head.

I'm not sure what it was. But suddenly, I was posing for photos with my natural hair. At the store, I searched for creams to twist my hair with. And online, I researched and found forums and new products specifically about and for natural hair. Something in me was changing and that transformation showed from the inside out.

The biggest symbol of conformity for African-American hair is the hot comb. In my earliest experiences with it before I moved to the flat iron, I would say the hot comb, or pressing comb as it is also known, represents the dreams and wishes of young girls to conform their hair to the world's standards.

We want our hair to blow in the wind, to flow down our backs, or to have that messy bun look when we pull it into an updo. Or we simply just want it to lay flat against the sides of our faces in a bob or rest gently by our collar bones. But where do all of these desires come from? Who has told us that the way our hair grows out of our heads is not beautiful, is not the so-called standard?

The looser our hair texture or the closer it is to brown or blond, our hair is accepted more easily. But we shouldn't have to conform our hair. I'm all about trying new styles and exploring the variety of extensions and clip-ins the market has to offer. But I'm also all about being me and loving *my* hair.

In a memoir by Sandra Uwiringiyimana, *How Dare the Sun Rise*, she writes that one of the first things she noticed after being relocated from Africa to America was that black girls wore their hair either in braids or weaves. No one had short, natural hair like her. She would be made fun of for not having "fake" hair. Eventually, she grew her hair long enough to wear braids. What struck me as I read this was how, in the Democratic Republic of Congo, where Sandra was from, wearing natural hair was a way of life. It wasn't looked down upon or ridiculed. It was just considered beautiful.

The earliest memory I have of my hair is Pink Lotion. You know the brand with the pastel pink bottle. It had an oily smell too. My mom would rub some between her hands and that's when the magic would happen and my dry hair would transform into clouds of soft puffs, expertly twisted or braided into sections with rubber bands and decorated with barrettes at the ends. I would fall asleep while getting my hair done. That's how relaxing it was. I still have distant memories of being carried, slung over one of my parents' shoulders, back to bed after a nightly styling session.

Over the years, my opinion of my hair would shift, but one thing would always remain the same. It was *my* hair. My responsibility. Not a burden but rather an opportunity. My hair and the choices I made to style it presented a pathway for me to express myself while also holding onto my ancestral roots. Pun intended. Of course, at the time, I did not think about it that way. I just wanted to be pretty. Beautiful in the eyes of others.

Sandra Cisneros has a vignette in *The House on Mango Street* called "The Family of Little Feet" where she describes three girls growing up. Despite the title, the point of the vignette couldn't be further from the topic of feet. As the story goes, receiving some older woman's heels in a bag, the girls decide to try them on. But as they walk through the neighborhood, they discover the cost of being "beautiful." After being mistaken for prostitutes by a local derelict, they dispose of the heels, admitting that they are tired of being beautiful.

In a way, their story mirrors mine with my natural hair. Somewhere along the way, I realized that wearing my hair naturally was okay and that by throwing off the world's idealization of what makes beautiful hair, I gradually lost interest in straightening my hair. Like the girls trying on heels and later discarding them, it can be tiring to live up to what is considered beautiful. Especially when it means changing your hair. Now, don't get me wrong: I love a stylish set of pumps. But the underlying message of the story still stuck. What image was I trying to create by straightening my hair and why was I doing it?

Middle school. The place where dreams are made or crushed. Hair really wasn't a thing in elementary. Maybe because I was less self-aware. It seemed to me no one really cared. Hair was hair. End of story.

Middle school changed things. I was hanging (let's be real, tagging along) with a clique that included my best friend. The main problem was that I was the only black girl. I still remember the photo taken at the middle school dance. You know the ones. The fake palm tree backdrop and cheap party streamers, glittering plastic and shiny. Off to the side in the photo was me wearing my hair pressed and curled from pink foam rollers. I didn't always wear my hair like this. I have a really pretty picture from middle school where my mom braided my hair and attached plastic seashells at the end of my front braids. I'm smiling in that photo like I am the happiest girl. But the dance was a special occasion. And special, for my hair, meant straight.

I think I was mainly trying to fit in. That all changed when my family moved from Indiana to North Carolina during the summer before I started high school. The South and the North are different places. It doesn't take me to tell you that though. Ask any Southerner and they will say the same. In North Carolina, besides being introduced to iced tea, I was also shown a world of diversity. My new high school had students from every culture under the sun. There was a radical shift in my thinking. I no longer had to adhere to the unspoken rules of one clique. I could wear my hair however I wanted and no one excluded me because of it.

First, I started off with long cornrows. My mom would take me to an African braiding shop not too far from my house. We could call and make an appointment ahead of time or else I'd have to wait before being able to be seen. This lasted only a short while. After one of my styling sessions, the shop manager changed the price and demanded that my mother pay more. The woman who had braided my hair had stood back, head bowed and docile, as if trapped herself. After my mom refused, she pushed me behind her to protect me from this man who was berating us for more money. We laugh about this memory together now, but in the moment, it was terrifying that this was happening in a braiding shop, a place where you are supposed to be able to be relaxed. My mom repeated that she was only going to pay the original price and we left. I never got my hair braided at that place again.

My sophomore year in high school is when the exciting experimenting started. With a little research, I found online forums and bloggers who talked about wearing their hair "natural." Though the blogs were great for a singular person's experience, I liked the forums best because they provided a window into a burgeoning online community of collective voices. It quickly became obvious what products people recommended as being the best. The market was a whole lot smaller then, but one or two brands were creating products for black hair. I had already started twisting my hair with some conditioner

I had lifted from my parents' bathroom, but after it made my scalp flaky with dandruff, I decided to purchase from newer, black-owned companies.

At a hotel on vacation somewhere, my brother called us all close to the TV. A new song played by Corinne Bailey Rae, an up-and-coming British pop singer, called "Put Your Records On." Both the song and the singer would forever transform my life and my internal perception of natural hair. The music video showed a brown-skinned woman riding her bike on a dirt pathway lined with fruitful trees, carefree. But my eyes were fixed on her hair. Kinky curls, coily and alive on top, and an upturned face with a smile that spilled over with joy. Corinne Bailey Rae was just the beginning.

From there, my natural hair journey took off. I twisted my hair faithfully and my mom even found a new stylist to do my twists for me. When my hair grew, we kept coming back. After a while, it got too expensive going every two weeks, so I began to teach myself the techniques. My senior year picture from high school is me in a twist out, smiling with all my natural hair in a spongy cloud. There were still times beauticians flat-ironed my hair (prom) or I wore a weave (my first year of college), but after suffering damage, I went back to styling my hair myself, naturally.

Although I kept my hair natural after joining the workforce, I did experience pressure for my hair to look "civilized" and tamed. Most of those stories are detailed in this book. But one thing that has never changed is my desire to be beautiful. Except now, instead of tossing my heels into a bag and hiding them away, I can proudly wear my pumps and my natural Afro together, fearlessly with a healthy measure of hair love because I have fully accepted and embraced God's divine love from above.

SHELIA'S HAIR STORY: FROM PLAITS TO 'FROS

My hair journey began as a little girl growing up in the early '60s in inner-city Chicago. My mother, whom I affectionately called "Madear" plaited my hair in eight braids with a small bang curled in front sitting atop my forehead. Everything about my hair was a chore. Washing my hair, with me on my knees, over the bathtub—a chore. Combing through what I heard referred to as "those naps" and "nappy edges" and that thick "kitchen" in the back of my head—a chore. I had to have it hot-combed to get those kinks out. A big chore. Through my childhood hair experiences, I was left thinking that straight was best and that the more naps that could be pressed out of your hair, the prettier your hair was.

My mother's personal hair journey influenced how she cared for my hair. Being thrice removed from slavery, my mother could clearly remember stories of her great-grandmother wearing tight scarves to hide the naps in the back along the neckline. She also recalled her mother (my grandmother) using the heavy steel pressing comb and steel curling irons over the gas stove. My mother had pictures of herself in her twenties with long thick pressed hair spiraling upward from her neckline to sit in a cascade of curls atop her crown. She only wanted my hair pretty and pressed like she knew.

Some of my favorite childhood memories were of Christmas time and looking through the Sears catalog books at all the dolls. I dreamed of having a doll with long blonde hair. I didn't realize that all the dolls with straight blonde hair were white. I just wanted the doll on the TV commercials. Then one special Christmas, I got the doll I wanted. I immediately began to fix the doll's hair like mine was fixed by my Madear. I parted the straight blonde hair and put hair grease between the parts and then tried to plait it, but it kept coming loose. So I added more grease. Next, I tried washing it. This made it worse. Needless to say, my doll's hair never got back like it originally was.

When I grew older and moved away to college in the mid-seventies, I began to see the big divide between my hair care and the hair care of white women. It just took too much time to care for my hair, especially when I had final exams, so I did a lot of fancy head wraps while in college. Also, the pressure to want to keep my hair straight and free of kinks grew. I moved from the chore of using the pressing comb to the ease of relaxers, which kept your hair straight longer. I began to experiment on my own with home box perms—those with no lye and those with lye. I also began to go to beauticians to put the relaxer in, some with their shops in homes and some at salons. It wasn't until I received a chemical burn from the relaxer not rinsing out well, causing a patch of my hair in the front to bald, that I decided to let my relaxer grow out and try the Jheri curl, which made my hair grow like crazy.

I was out of college and married in the late eighties when I had my last Jheri curl because the products needed to keep it moisturized left a wet, messy residue on everything, especially pillowcases when that plastic bag moved off my head at night. By then, our first child—our son—had been born. He loved to grab hold of my wet, sleek, Jheri-curled hair and I decided it was time to let the hair chemicals go and go natural. I wore an Afro, although I still preferred my hair straight. By the time both our daughters had been born in the early nineties, I still held lingering beliefs that straight was prettier, and from time to time, I would still hot comb my own hair.

By the time my daughters (Melissa—oldest, and Sylvia—youngest) were school age, I likewise began pressing their hair and fighting with that doggone kitchen hot comb like my Madear had done with me.

"Hold your head down! Don't lift it or I might accidentally burn your neck."

"Keep it down! Just a little longer. There! It looks great." *Sizzle. Sizzle.* Straight. Smiles. "All done!"

My personal hair journey affected the way I approached my daughters' hair care. I especially wanted their hair to be seamlessly straight with no real chore.

Melissa's hair took easily to pressing and became straight after a hot press. Her hair was so thick and coarse that even after a good pressing, it would hold any curl shape imaginable and even stand up on top of her head. Sylvia's hair didn't take to pressing as easily. Her hair would take too much heat to get it straight and I was afraid of burning it, so I'd give it a light press, and sure enough, within hours, it was back to its natural state. Also, Sylvia resisted sitting for the "hot comb business" as she called it and I grew tired of fighting with her over it, so I just left her hair with its natural springiness.

I knew relaxers would cause breakage if not properly applied or cared for; however, I was still partial to the Jheri curl since it had made my hair grow and my perspective was that long without nappy is pretty. So, when our eldest daughter wanted a curl when she was in her teens, I didn't object. Melissa got her curl and her hair grew, but by the time she was ready for her high school prom, she had grown out her curl and gotten a relaxer. The style looked gorgeous on her, with the updo the beautician had given her. She looked so princess-like that I dismissed the fact that relaxing her hair could easily lead to hair breakage if not regularly taken care of.

Later, in her twenties, Melissa went back to relaxers. Why not? No objections were said by me. In fact, I encouraged the short style that the beautician was giving her. At the time, not only was he relaxing her hair but he was also gluing in the straight bangs that flowed on the side of her head. The glue-in was applied directly to her crown and not to a mesh cap. Eventually, my daughter began to see the hair loss and the balding in her crown.

I often sob over my daughter Melissa's hair loss. I have blamed myself for not giving her wise hair advice. The damage from the glue-in tracks, along with the tight braid styles, along with the relaxers all contributed to my daughter's CCCA. My heart broke when I went with her to the dermatologist and saw the breakage and balding.

When I think about my hair journey, I know it influenced how I cared for my daughters' hair. Just like my mother's hair journey influenced how she cared for my hair. I weep with silent tears over what I could have done differently and regret what I did not do right.

But now, I'm liberated in my thinking about my hair and its care. I now accept and love the feel and touch of my hair. This liberation came about as my younger daughter, Sylvia, began practices with natural herbs and oils to help Melissa begin treating her CCCA. Sylvia's determination showed Melissa and me both the beauty of natural hair. Now I see my natural Afro hair as beautifully endowed by God. All three of us are together on this journey of accepting and caring for our natural God-given hair. And we are loving it!

SPIRITUAL
& HISTORICAL ROOTS

In an interview promoting Hulu's docuseries *The Hair Tales*, Tracee Ellis Ross said, "I believe that hair is like a portal into our souls . . . Hair care is self-care . . . It connects us to our legacy, it connects us to our history, it connects us to our community, and our family, and our own personal stories." Hair, like every other part of our body, is sacred. Our Afro-textured hair is more than just a physical feature; it has something to say about our history. Our natural hair journeys mean going back to hairstyles our ancestors wore centuries ago, like expertly braided cornrows. And in the spirit of Sankofa, an Akan word that literally translates to "it is not taboo to fetch what is at risk of being left behind," we return to our roots to get what is in danger of being left behind in order to mend our present and manifest our future.

As the highest point of a person's body, hair was thought to be a conduit for spiritual communication in precolonial West African societies. Certain *orishas*, or intermediary gods and goddesses in Yoruba mythology, were described as skilled hairdressers; their worshippers appropriately wore specific braided hairstyles.[1] The idea that hair growth and spiritual symbolism are entwined isn't unique to African belief systems. Sikh men and women keep their hair long to follow principles that are part of their religion. In Indigenous American cultures, long hair is linked to both a person's spiritual energy and her cultural identity.[2]

Such beliefs have Biblical histories also. One of the most intimate acts of worship in the Ancient Near East was the taking of the Nazarite vow (Numbers 6:1–21) to abstain from cutting one's hair for a specific number of days, after which the Nazirite would—in a holy "big chop"—shave his or her head and subsequently burn the hair as an offering.

From being symbolized as a supernaturally sensitive antenna in some cultures to serving as a dedicated sacrifice in others, hair is, and has always been, more than just hair.

Hairstyles said a lot about the identity of those who wore them in fifteenth-century African societies. Within the kingdoms of the Yoruba, Wolof, Mandingo, and Mende, hairstyles were a complex, unspoken language that communicated one's social standing, marital status, religious affiliation, ethnic group, wealth, surname or clan identity, and age.[3] The art of interweaving your identity into your hair is still a contemporary African practice. For a woman from the Himba tribe in northwestern Namibia, the hairstyle she wears as a young girl is different from the one she wears when she's ready to be courted, which is different from the one she wears as a married woman, which is different from the one she wears as a married woman with kids.[4] Hairstyles always change with the stages of a woman's life.

The Blessing of InHAIRitance: Ancient Hairstyles of Today

One afternoon, Melissa and I visited a local art museum. After a refreshing walk by the museum gardens and a gurgling fountain, we went to tour the art exhibits inside. Although we toured several different floors, there was one piece in the African art galleries that garnered our attention. Once we had viewed wooden figures and masks and chit-chatted about the textiles and ceramics, we both noticed a glass case in the middle of the exhibit.

The description read:

> *"Mbukushu people. Botswana or Namibia. Woman's headdress. In the past Mbukushu women wore beautiful wigs that were fixed into their hair with braids. For years, mothers would prepare young girls to wear the heavy headdresses by oiling their hair and braiding it with beads & other accessories."*

The first thing I thought was: *Wait! So, we wore wigs in Africa?!* Apparently yes . . . and beautiful, traditional wigs at that. But instead of being called "wigs" or "hair pieces," they were known as headdresses. A little further research led me to learn that different African tribal groups have their own unique headdresses special to them. Depending on the tribal group, the headdress can be symbolic of a young female transitioning into puberty, marriage, or motherhood. For example, Himba women wear Ehando wigs and Ekori bonnets or crowns at different stages in their lives.

My sister and I were amazed by this discovery. Perhaps, weaves, wigs, and hair pieces connect African Americans today with the customs of our ancestors. Maybe we can glean something else from this information as well both about ourselves and our hair. Our hair is not only something to celebrate, embrace, and nurture but it also holds ancestral significance that shines the spotlight on customs and traditions.

The Burden of Legacy: Four Hundred Years of Hair Trauma

Black people using innumerable products to stretch, enhance, or alter the texture of our hair is rooted in a history of lack.

Enslaved African men and women, robbed of the tools and oils they used to craft elaborate, complex hairstyles in their own societies resorted to using Western oil-based substitutes such as butter, bacon fat, goose grease, and even axle grease. Black women mixed lye and potatoes together to create a caustic hair-straightening concoction.[5]

Four hundred years later, researchers have only begun to make the connections between the use of chemical hair straighteners and uterine cancer, which, though a rare form of cancer, appears at higher rates among black women than women of other ethnicities.[6] Moreover, contemporary hair care products for Afro-textured hair use the supposed deficiency of natural hair as a promotional tactic, masking the wolf of denigration in the sheep's clothing of guarantees to make Afro hair more defined, shinier, manageable, or "tame." Because of such product promises, black women are lured into spending millions upon millions of dollars on beauty products.[7]

In addition to social conditioning, we face pressure to change our hair to appear more professional, or in other words, acceptable to a majority-white society. Whether in school, a 9-to-5 job, or the White House, black women and men are discriminated against for wearing traditional natural hairstyles. The CROWN Act (Creating a Respectful and Open World for Natural Hair) is a law—still not passed by Congress at the date of this book's publication—that specifically redresses this form of racism by prohibiting discrimination based on hair texture or hairstyles.

Because the legacy of hair trauma that began during enslavement continues today, black women and our natural hair have endured the trauma of chemical straighteners, damaging hair products, and societal discrimination for centuries.

How we wear our hair matters (to the women around us).

Sometimes I (Sylvia) wonder if this natural hair journey is worth it. Face it. Depending on where you live, you might have the problem of limited stylists or overpriced styling tools—or maybe it's neither of those things. Maybe it's just you are a solo act. You are the only one wearing your hair like this, and in the mirror, you have to affirm yourself daily that, yes, kinky roots really are beautiful after all and, no, you don't need a weave.

When I find my hands itching to add in crochet curls or clip-ins and it's not just for a protective style, I have to ask myself, "Am I hiding?" "Am I changing and shaping my hair to fit society's expectations or am I fearlessly being me?"

Sometimes wearing your own hair can inspire others. Like that one time I showed up after Labor Day break at work, rockin' an Afro puff, and wouldn't you know, another black coworker was rockin' one too. Or like when you see a gorgeous Afro up close in real life, and you smile, cheering and celebrating the beauty of differences.

Those moments are memorable to me. I think something we have been taught and learned is that we must hide our different hair textures. That "kinky" is just something that needs to be straightened and curls were made for a flat iron, hissing heat. But these are lies we tell ourselves in order to climb into the box created by others that dictates what is considered beautiful.

I remember getting my hair flat ironed. Was it an operation! My strong kinks would not yield to the hot comb or flat iron. It took multiple times to get my hair to hang straight which was damaging to my hair. In addition to the flat iron I can still see the faces of the boys in my science class who turned and looked at me because I showed up with straight hair. But what about the times I wore braids or twists? I was equally beautiful then. But I was blinded by what the magazine covers and TV shows sold as beautiful, and that meant straight hair was the fairest of them all.

Today, when I see another woman with natural hair, I beam with enthusiasm and I feel uplifted and affirmed with a sense of pride. It's validating to wear my hair just as it is. Even if I don't have a lot of hair or even if it's not perfect, simply expressing my uniqueness is enough. It makes a statement. When I see another woman with natural hair or a scarf, it is like seeing a beautiful reflection of myself. We inadvertently say: this is our space and we can be ourselves here. One woman influences another.

Ways to Uplift Other Natural Hair Women

Be kind. Encourage one another. Compliments stay with you, so give them freely. It doesn't cost you anything. If you see a style or look you like, say it.

Be sensitive. Be ready to listen to how another woman feels about her hair before talking about yourself. Being a good listener shows empathy, and who knows: as you trade stories, you may have shared experiences!

Be open. Be willing to offer tips, realizing that everyone's hair is different. Share books (like this one) or even schedule regular hair checks or updates to track your progress. Everyone needs a little community and encouragement in their life about their hair.

THE MAKER'S TOOLS

When I was growing up, there used to be a drawer in our family home where we kept the hairdressing tools. The hair picks and combs with gapped-tooth grins. Those pink, puffy rollers that had coils of black hair stubbornly snagged in the plastic corners. Bobby pins and that grease-marked box of wafer-thin papers Mom used to wrap around the rollers before wrapping our pressed bangs around them. Doing our hair requires specific tools—the right tools.

In the same way, if we are to detangle the historical and personal trauma done to our natural hair both by others and ourselves, we must use the right spiritual tools–our Maker's tools.

We are all at different places in our hair journeys. You may be facing health issues or medical treatments that affect your hair. You may be at menopausal age, which affects your hair's texture, elasticity, or growth. Or you may be experiencing alopecia, resulting from harsh chemicals, damaging hairstyles, or genetics. You could just be having a bad hair day—or season.

The clarion call of this book is to see our natural hair as made in the image of God. We pray that this book sits on your desk during your quiet time, on your lap while you're getting your hair done, and that it serves as a spiritual guidebook along your personal natural hair journey.

It's a journey full of twists and turns, but don't worry—like Afro hair, it always treks up. It's a journey we traveled together through Melissa's alopecia diagnosis and continued healing, both of her scalp and her hair esteem. It's a journey that led us to write this book so that you can take your first step with us and we can testify together that our individual, coily hair textures are unique, God-created crowns.

REFLECTIONS TO FIND THE DIVINE IN MY NATURAL HAIR

The hair is the richest ornament of women.

—Dr. Martin Luther King, Jr.

1   Transform My Thinking Instead of My Hair

Do not conform to the pattern of this world, but be transformed by the renewing of your mind.
—*Romans 12:2 NIV*

The concept of leaving [my hair] the way it grew from my head was simply inconceivable.
—*Emma Dabiri,* Twisted

I (Shelia) have been married for forty years and now have three adult children. After I birthed my middle child, I hadn't lost the "baby fat" and I felt less attractive, dissatisfied with my overall appearance. It was popular at that time for black ladies to dye their hair blondish-red. I thought, "If I do that, I will feel better about myself."

My ebony black hair came out sun-blonde yellow! Sunblonde yellow against my deep mahogany skin complexion!

My husband took one look at me and said, "What did you do to your hair now? I wish you would just leave it alone. I like it as it is!"

The dye had damaged it so badly that, after about a week, my hair broke off. I had to wear a wig until it grew back.

When you are unhappy with yourself, you want to look like someone else. Wanting to look like someone else is often at the root of bad hair choices. You want to conform to the image of others. What you must do is be *transformed*.

Renew your way of thinking about your hair. Your hair is uniquely yours. It's HAIR today. Take care of it so that it is not GONE tomorrow. Trying to conform to an image that is not you is destructive. Just be yourself. Renew your mind to accept your natural hair.

Lord, thank you for my hair. Change my thinking so I love my natural hair.

2   Affirming My Hair

> [They] make you feel like there's something wrong with
> you if you're not relaxed, or they'll say things like, "If you
> ever straightened it, imagine how long it would be." But,
> I'm like, "I don't want straight hair!"
> —Corinne Bailey Rae

I (Sylvia, here) was walking downtown with my best friend
when a young guy with locks called out to me, "Hey, I really
like your hair!" Surprised at the compliment—my twist out was
wind-blown and fluffed out from the humidity—I managed to
say a simple, "Thank you."

Over the years of wearing my natural hair, I have received
many reactions, most pleasant, some awkward.

As the online natural hair community has grown, I've
noticed the pressure women with natural hair place upon one
another. No longer is it good enough to just have natural
hair; one must have it styled and displayed a certain way. On
blogs and videos, women chat about the "problem" of hair
"shrinkage," liking their hair better when it is stretched and
appears longer. Whether you prefer stretched natural hair over
un-stretched natural hair, women with natural hair need not
begin a new conformity: the thinking that unless hair is styled
a certain way, it isn't as beautiful as others in the natural hair
community who have hair of different textures, various fashion
preferences, and many personal tastes.

Idolizing another woman's hair—even if her hair is natural—
can cause you to harm your hair and emotionally damage your
personal confidence. Time spent musing about how beautiful

another woman's hair is robs you of time. Focus on enhancing your own natural hair, uplifting your self-image. Believing that you can buy the products and follow the exact steps of your hair idol to make your hair better and more like hers is setting yourself up for disappointment and potential hair and scalp damage. Begin appreciating the attributes and characteristics of your own hair before buying a product.

When you see another woman who has natural hair you admire, sincerely compliment her and learn what you can use from her, without tearing down or demeaning your own hair.

God, I want to overcome my anxiety about my hair. Show me how to begin believing you have made my hair beautiful. Help me overcome comparing myself with others, even others who have natural hair.

3   Hair Identity

*I don't just wear locs. They are a part of me. A gift to me.
They mean something to me.*
                                —Ava DuVernay

A man who cuts his hair is like a tree without leaves.
                                —Rastafarian Proverb

"I'm going to cry," Andrew Johnson said to his high school
wrestling coach, "but cut it." Andrew had been seconds away
from participating in his first match on the evening of December
19, 2018, when a white referee said that the sixteen-year-
old's dreadlocks were "unnatural" and demanded that Andrew
cut his hair or forfeit the match. This same referee had been
involved in racist incidents in the past, but had never received
more than a brief suspension that was later overturned. With
his school's ninth-straight division title on the line, Andrew
was forced to stand in full view of a packed gymnasium, his
family watching, as a white trainer chopped off his coiffed
dreadlocks a fistful at a time with a pair of kitchen scissors.
The lifeless locks fell to the mat around Andrew's shoes. The
referee, satisfied, finally allowed the match to begin. At the
end of the meet, alone with his mom, Andrew broke down in
tears.[1] He'd won the match, but lost a part of himself.

   Like a crown is to a king, a regal mane is to a lion, or leaves
are to a tree, hair is a visually powerful symbol of identity.
Thousands of years ago, Nazirites, men and women who
dedicated themselves to God by letting their hair grow,
also believed that hair was inseparable from the identity of a

person. The Hebrew root word for "nazirite" translates to "an unpruned vine."[2] Like a Nazirite centuries ago, cutting the hair, or "pruning the vine," for a black person is the same as being cut off from the symbol of one's identity.

The most famous Nazirite who ever lived was Samson. Unlike other men and women who took the vow to become Nazirites for a period of time, Samson was a Nazirite "from the womb" (Judges 13:5 NIV), his entire life dedicated to God even before he was born to free his nation from oppressive enemies. As he grew up and into the purpose God had placed on his life, performing superhuman feats throughout the land, Samson wore his unshorn hair in seven long, thick braids (Judges 16:19 NIV).

He was stronger than any other foe because no razor had ever touched his head—until his lover, Delilah, betrayed him. After she had Samson's braids chopped off, Samson awoke to find himself shaved, weakened, and surrounded by his enemies. They gouged out his eyes and enslaved him in their prison. It would seem like Samson's purpose, like his hair, was lost after that. "But," the Bible tells us, "the hair on his head began to grow again" (Judges 16:22 NIV). Samson eventually vanquished all his enemies, freeing his nation from their oppressive rule, and fulfilling the glorious purpose God had for him all along.

The referee who forced Andrew to cut off his hair didn't know that the viral video of what happened would become part of a movement that grew into the CROWN Act (Creating a Respectful and Open World for Natural Hair), the first American bill to prohibit race-based hair discrimination against a person's hair texture or hairstyle.[3] Andrew was robbed of a part of himself when a trainer chopped off his dreadlocks. But while the adults in that situation took away the *symbol* of his identity, they could not take away his identity nor stop his experience from opening the way to freedom from hairstyle discrimination for other black boys and girls.

Majority-white society says that Afro-textured hair and hairstyles are *not standard, unprofessional, messy,* and *unnatural.* It demands that black people straighten, change, or cut off our natural hair. The result of this pressure is the weakening of our self-esteem. But we have a secret. Like Samson, the strength of our identity is ultimately not in our hair but in our close relationship with the God who created us and our natural hair. God said we are fearfully and wonderfully made (Psalm 139:14 NIV). God said our hair is *very good* (Genesis 1:31 NIV). Because of this, when we face hair discrimination, we can do what our hair does: Stand up. Grow in the knowledge that our hair, like we ourselves, can never be cut off from the love of God (Romans 8:38–39).

Dear God, I will see my hair from your point-of-view and stand up to hair discrimination.

4 Rest for a While

> "We live in a culture that so celebrates certain kinds of beauty . . . that we slowly start to lose ourselves because we start masking our real self and acquiescing to what someone else has determined was beautiful."
>
> —Priscilla Shirer

Growing up as a little girl in the early sixties, I (Shelia) would see many commercials on television, advertising hair that didn't look like mine. Catchphrases like *bouncing and beautiful, soft and caressing, swooshing and pleasant to touch* were always used to describe straight hair. These words communicated to me as a child that this kind of hair was desirable and *good*. Whenever I heard Madear say, "Shelia, it's time to do your hair," I would contrast the straight hair of women in those commercials to my hair, which needed "to get the knots out," and think of my hair time as a big chore.

I continued seeing my hair as a chore well into my early twenties and attempted many ways to straighten it, from hot-combing, to flat-ironing, to using home box relaxers, to Jheri curls, to beauty shop relaxers. My hair experienced shock after shock all in an effort to get the knots out.

My hair journey began to take a different route once I got married and had my first child. I began asking myself, "How can I get over this feeling that my hair is a burden?" I got over it by agreeing with the words in Matthew 11.

I knew it was time to rest my hair and renew my focus on spiritual things. I began to see my natural hair not as a chore but as a privilege to honor God in an act of praise. (See 22S

"Combating Hair Care Fatigue" for tips for letting your hair rest.)

Whenever I am tempted to see my natural hair as a burden, I know that it's time to rest and renew my focus.

Jesus, I come to you to help me rest from the desire of wishing that my hair is any way other than the way you designed it. Thank you for giving me rest in you.

5 Happy Hair

My frame was not hidden from You, When I was made in secret, And skillfully wrought . . . Your eyes have seen my unformed substance.

—Psalms 139:14–17 NASB

These verses from Psalm 139 were not what many of us heard about ourselves growing up and especially about our hair. Many of us heard the phrase, "Girl, your edges are so nappy!"

As a little girl, whenever I (Shelia) heard the phrase "nappy," it made me think that my hair needed to be fixed or straightened. My "nappy" hair was not acceptable. From hot-combing to relaxing to Jheri curling—the goal was to straighten my nappy hair. I could only be happy with my hair once it was straightened. I deeply regret my partiality to these processes of straight hair because they led me to want my oldest daughter to have straight hair, which eventually contributed to her hair loss from CCCA.

Changing our thinking about nappy hair begins by understanding that we are fearfully and wondrously made by our Creator. We don't have to straighten anything God has created coiled or wavy or any other configuration. Many of us have been on a journey of nappy to happy when our God-given hair has been *happy hair* all along.

A round of applause and thanksgiving to you, God, because you made me incredibly wonderful without reservation, including my hair. You are my Maker and you created me as an amazing work of awe when only your eyes could see my unformed substance. Nothing about me was out of your mind or hidden from sight when you skillfully crafted every inch of me. You think of me as priceless. I know that you made me not as an afterthought but by intentional design. I am a phenomenal treasure of your choice, and this makes me happy with my hair! God, you make me feel so satisfied with myself. I am happy with myself because you are happy with me!

6 Throwing Out the Magazines

> *Whoopi Goldberg looked like me, she had hair like mine,*
> *she was dark like me. I'd been starved for images of my-*
> *self. I'd grown up watching a lot of American TV.*
> —*Lupita Nyong'o*

I (Sylvia) often look for chick flicks featuring African-American women. When I was younger, it didn't much matter that these movies did not center women who looked like me. Today, it matters a lot.

How we see ourselves and our natural hair is influenced by the images we view on TV or in magazines. The standard of beauty we see means changing our natural hair to fit a certain image. If we try to imitate what the media industry projects, we will rarely be comfortable with our natural hair. Brainwashing happens when our image of beauty is determined by the media and we think our natural hair is not attractive.

If you can mentally check the box next to these scenarios, you may need to take a step back and examine your definition of beauty for your natural hair:

- I regularly use damaging styling practices so my hair will look a certain way. (See Salon Chair Session 4S "Damaging Styling Practices.")
- I don't feel beautiful unless I have "that" style.
- All my hair crushes or celebrities have hair that looks nothing like my hair texture.
- I'm afraid to wear a style with my own natural hair.

I admit to myself that I do not feel comfortable wearing my natural hair. I want to wear my own natural hair without worrying about other people's expectations or media images. I commit to learning how to style it myself or to give it some recovery time to become natural again so I can wear my natural hair in all its glory.

7   Crowns

You have given me the heritage of those who fear, revere,
and *honor Your name.*

—*Psalms 61:5 AMPC*

When I (Shelia) think of wearing a crown in heaven, I think of my mother, Madear. She loved wearing big church hats. She had one for every church occasion—from spring Women's Day programs to summer weddings to winter banquets—in unique colors, shapes, and styles. Those hats crowned her head with regal beauty.

It makes me smile when I think of her wearing one of her crowns and the eternal crown she now wears in heaven because of the life she lived on earth. She was passionate about her faith and a witness to others. Madear accepted Christ as her personal savior at the age of twelve. She was a phenomenal, spiritual woman, fearless and courageous.

When she got older, Madear experienced hair loss on her scalp at the crown of her head. She never shared her feelings about her hair loss with me. She just continued to live a determined, purposeful, spiritual life, wearing her hats, set on a mission of caring for others and introducing them to Christ.

As I feel pain about my daughter Melissa's alopecia, I do wish Madear had shared her feelings about her hair loss with me so I could share her story in her own words with Melissa, who looks so much like my mother. In fact, when Melissa was an infant, I told Madear that so closely did Melissa resemble Madear's features—even down to how she grimaces and holds her mouth—it was like seeing her as a baby.

When I look at my daughter's crown and see the alopecia looking back at me, I wish I could erase the pain she feels. I consider how Madear must have felt, wearing her church hats. When I see Melissa wearing scarves because of the alopecia, I feel she has a hidden crown, unrevealed phenomenal spirituality, fearlessness, and courage. The strength of my mother resonates within my daughter Melissa.

Dear Lord, I have struggled so long with my own pain and guilt over my daughter's alopecia. I come to you and release this grief to you.

8 In Touch with My Hair

I feel that the kinks, curls, or tight coils in Afro hair is
beautiful and unique. No other race on this planet has
hair like ours—that makes me proud.
                    —*Monica Millner, author of* Natural & Free:
                                        Journey to Natural Beauty

A lot of us as black women don't touch our hair often because we go from protective styles to beauticians' shops. Not regularly touching our hair can emotionally disconnect us from our hair, robbing us of pride and love for it—and ourselves. This problem has historical roots. During centuries of enslavement in America, black women covered their hair with head rags, deprived of the time and tools needed to perform daily hair care practices by their enslavers.[1]

Touching our natural hair unearths feelings, often self-esteem that has been shackled for far too long. Then five-year-old Jacob Philadelphia, who asked to touch President Barack Obama's hair because he wanted to see if they had the same hair texture, is an example that speaks volumes.

When was the last time you allowed your fingers to pleasurably touch your natural hair and massage your scalp? Next time you touch your natural hair, know that its unique texture was handcrafted by God, and that it is *good* hair.

Thank you that I can feel the length and depth and
height and width of your love for me, Lord, by taking
pleasure in your awesome creativity of my hair texture.
This helps me to be in touch with my hair.

9 *God honors my hair.*

> *How beautiful you are, my darling! Oh, how beautiful! . . . Your hair is like a flock of goats descending from the hills of Gilead.*
>
> —*Song of Solomon 4:1 NIV*

The Song of Solomon is about God's love for us. Solomon describes his bride and her hair. We sense the bridegroom's tenderness toward his bride in his description of her hair, which he compares to "a flock of goats." Goat hair, or wool, is soft, thick, short, and curly.

In our culture today, it's hard to see having "hair like wool" as a positive characteristic. The word "wool" in relation to thick, curly, short hair has a racist, traumatic history. During slavery, African Americans' hair texture was just one of many physical attributes—like the hue of our skin and our facial features—that was dehumanized. Enslavers would refer to enslaved peoples' hair as wool to associate it with animals and differentiate it from their own straight hair texture.[1]

In God's Word, though, comparing hair to wool has a positive meaning. In Song of Solomon, thick, curly hair that is likened to wool is passionately described as lovely. In some versions, it even refers to our woolly hair as like a shimmering, black, wavy fleece. In Song of Solomon 4:1, AMPC, it says, "Your hair makes me think of the black, wavy fleece of a flock." In Song of Solomon 4:1 (AMP), it says, "Your hair is like the shimmering black fleece of a flock of Arabian goats."

God made our woolly hair, and it is so lovely that it is described in the most intimate, detailed description of love in the Bible.

If you have trouble imagining your thick, kinky, curly, wiry, short hair as a "flock of goats" leaping down the slopes of Gilead, remember that, like the bridegroom in Song of Solomon, God loves and cherishes your hair.

God, thank you for showing me that the way you made my natural hair is beautiful. I will wear my hair natural—even when others fail to see its beauty or tell me otherwise—as a response to your tender love for me.

10   When I'm the Only Afro in the Room

Having Black hair is unique in that Black women change up styles a lot. You can walk down one street block in New York City and see 10 different hairstyles that Black women are wearing: straight, curls, shortcuts, braids—we really run the gamut.

—Queen Latifah

I (Sylvia) had only planned to attend the new Bible study once or twice. But one time quickly turned to four. I liked the vibe and the feeling of being surrounded by other Christians. The only problem was that as I looked around, I was the only one in the room wearing an Afro.

I had taken to fluffing my hair out and letting my natural hair do its thing. If it became puffy—no big deal. Rain? Bring it on. I couldn't care less about my hair being perfect because I wanted to be myself and express my uniqueness. But as I noticed the straight blonde and brown hair of others, I began to feel like I stood out in the *wrong* way. Before the worship music started, I stopped in the mirror to admire my gold hoops and Afro and wondered, *Was just being me okay or did I need to change my hair to blend in?*

When you're the only person with natural hair, it can be easy to become insecure. Take a moment to step back and assess your feelings and your actions.

Ask yourself: *Why don't I wear my hair natural? Is it to please other people?* The best reason to wear your natural hair is that the uniqueness of your hair glorifies God, your Creator.

Next: *What does beauty mean to me?* Instead of looking for definitions of what is beautiful from the latest trends or what's popular, determine what natural hairstyle looks best on you for your face shape.

Finally: Focus on what God says about you as a person and your hair. You are a child of God. Always welcome your Creator's presence.

> *When I am the only Afro in the room, the only one with natural hair in a room, no matter where I am—whether it be in church, a workplace, or another public space—I will wear my God-given crown proudly and do what's healthy for my hair instead of waiting for people's praises or fearing their rebukes.*

11 My hair is like a garden.

All by itself it sprouts, and the soil produces a crop; first the green stem, then the head on the stalk, and then the fully developed grain in the head.

—Mark 4:28 TPT

Imagine a vegetable garden sprouting up at the peak of summer after the soil has been treated with peat moss, which softens it, and fertilizer, which adds nutrients. What a wonderful sight. For a gardener, it is exciting to see growth because the gardener knows a harvest is coming.

Sometimes, soil can be hard and less fertile, so it takes more than a conventional hoe to break it up. Yet, the gardener doesn't give up but takes a tiller to help manipulate and coax the tight, hard soil. Next, the soil is nurtured and pampered until the tiny plants begin to pop up. First the green stem, then the head on the stalk, and then the fully developed fruit or veggie.

Our hair is like a garden and needs nurturing, nutrients, sunshine, and water. Like garden soil can be hard and unresponsive, our hair pores may be resistant; so, a strand of hair struggles to push through. Maybe your hair is damaged and breaking off excessively or you're just getting tired of "managing" it. Maybe it's turning gray or growing thinner and you feel your glory days of having a full head of beautiful hair are behind you. Whatever season your hair is in, like a garden, it needs constant attention. We each find what works best for our hair and become disciplined in its care to avoid barrenness. Withholding this attention from your scalp and roots is like neglecting the condition of a garden's soil. Be watchful of changes and be intentional to use the right nutrients. It is satisfying to see your hair growth and even more gratifying to know that the specific care and nourishment given to your hair impacts this growth.

And just as a garden sprouts its crop because it's given divine attention from our Creator God who lavishes it with the needed sun and rain, we too are cared for by God. God never stops caring about us. So, whatever stage your hair is in, nurture it like a garden and know that your hair glorifies a holy God who loves it just as it is no matter where you are in your journey.

Please help me, Lord, to honor you in keeping up with my hair care and nourishing my hair like a garden.

12 *No Longer Ashamed*

> *"Today I was preaching, and I could feel my wig slipping. My message was more important to me than maintaining my appearance, so I took it off, locked in, and kept preaching."*
>
> —*Pastor Sarah Jakes*

When a teacher at the school where I (Shelia) was the principal stepped back into her classroom, she had to immediately quiet the gale of laughter. Two third-grade girls were teasing another girl in class about her hair. Her mom had not taken her to the salon to get her relaxer touched up; lots of new growth had come in and the edges and nape line showed thick natural hair. The teacher stopped the teasing and later came to a meeting with the mom, daughter, and me to ensure that this student felt good about her natural hair. Throughout the meeting, the teacher referred to this student as beautiful, repeatedly told her the other students were wrong for teasing her, and said, "You have nothing to be ashamed of about your hair." I saw the reaction of this third-grade girl. She moved from holding her head down to sitting up straight and smiling at us. The mom, too, reacted favorably to the teacher's positive comments.

In 2 Timothy, Paul writes about never again feeling ashamed because he believed in God and therefore knew who he was. God elevated him above all feelings of shame.

Perhaps you struggle with feeling ashamed of your natural hair. You may feel discontent and discomfort about your hair texture or hair length. Or you may be ashamed of hair loss or signs of alopecia. This shame is intensified when you are inundated with media that doesn't affirm Afro-textured natural hair.

Reflect on who God says you are and rejoice, without shame, over your hair because God created it and the Creator is rejoicing over you.

My Creator God, I want to never again feel ashamed about my hair.

13 Hands off my hair!

Don't touch my hair.

—Solange Knowles

The 2016 song "Don't Touch My Hair" by Solange Knowles caught the world off guard. I mean, really: black women have been saying the phrase "Don't touch my hair" for years, but to actually have a song that puts it out there so well—we couldn't ask for more. The essence of the song is that our natural hair is intrinsically connected to our souls and when someone treats it like it is exotic, wild, or a circus roadshow, we have the right to hold our heads high and demand dignity. Solange, in the music video, dramatically flips her beaded braids with a confidence that can only inspire.

While we all wish to be as self-assured about our natural hair as the song describes, sometimes you can't decide what's getting you down about your hair. You get looks and stares and the occasional dismissive glance that makes your stomach drop and your nerves quiver. No one should ever make you feel ashamed of your hair, including yourself, by internalizing the messages around you.

When you find it difficult to notice or acknowledge positive responses to your natural hair, you dismiss compliments, wave them off, or act like you didn't hear. More than once, I (Sylvia) have been told, "I like your hair" when I have worn a twist out and the comment caught me off guard. I felt my defenses go up. Because even though I liked my hair and thought it looked cute that morning, having someone else, especially someone of a different race, compliment me was bewildering. We live in a media world where our natural hair is not celebrated. It can make us feel so insecure or ashamed, we can't receive a compliment.

Then there are the looks. We've all seen them. You walk into a room, feeling cute with your new hairstyle only to catch a pointed gaze that is not-too-friendly. Or that quick glance that tries to act like it wasn't staring when it definitely *was* staring. The looks might make you regret wearing your natural hairstyle or change it the next day.

Changing your hair, second-guessing your beauty based on people's perceptions, or internalizing negative messages so you want to hide your natural hair texture or make it looser or do whatever will make your hair more appealing to your audience, all stop you from loving your hair as it is.

Instead, change the narrative. No matter how people respond to your natural hair, do not be ashamed. Make the choice to love what your Creator made. Know your natural hair is beautiful and that it suits you. Don't bend to what others think. Embrace the beauty you have and walk into any room with your head of natural hair held high.

Lord, please help me to love my hair the way you created it. Show me how to wear my natural hair with inner confidence.

14   We're on this hair journey together.

"There was a lady at our church . . . and she would do my hair and speak into my life. She would encourage me. . . . It wasn't even like all the time but when she did it, it meant the world to me and I could live off those moments for a long, long time."

—*Nicole C. Mullen*

That day when I (Shelia) accompanied my daughter Melissa to her dermatologist appointment to see about her hair loss, I whispered a prayer to God to give us what we needed. I felt a grave sense of guilt, along with the pain of seeing her hair loss. *What could I have done differently? Maybe if I hadn't put her braids in so tight when she was a little girl . . . Maybe I shouldn't have let her get that perm and weave in when she was a teenager . . . Or maybe I should have done a better job selecting hair products.*

My daughter was not aware of the roller coaster of emotions I was having as the dermatologist examined her scalp. All she could see was that I was there with her, that I was there for her, no matter what. She recognized that she was not alone in her journey.

I transferred the pain, guilt, grief, and helplessness to prayers, knowing God hears and answers and always readily supplies our needs. During my daughter's examination, I pledged to God I would work in harmony with my prayers, to do whatever I needed to do to help my daughter gain back whatever hair she could.

That meant intentionally coming alongside her in her hair routine. My daughter knows she's not alone, that she has an intercessor in me and the love and support of the rest of her family. She's stronger because we are all on this hair journey together.

The Lord's Prayer (Matthew 6:9–13 NRSV) was given by Christ as our model for prayer. Jesus is with us on our path of hair loss and we should never hesitate to bring it to the Lord, who tends to our every need. God sees our pain and nothing is beyond the reach and concern of our Provider.

*Dear God, I come to you with my hair loss (or_____).
I invite you to be with me on my hair journey, directing
me along the way.*

15 Work it, girl!

If Michelle Obama had natural hair when Barack Obama was running for president, he would not have won . . . because her natural hair would have signified certain things to people. It would signify that she's some sort of militant.

—*Chimamanda Ngozi Adichie*

Let me keep my hair straight. . . . Let's get health care passed.

—*Former First Lady Michelle Obama*

I love how Michelle is now wearing her natural hair and I understand why she didn't do this while Barack was running for or while he served as president. In an article for *Essence* Magazine, writer Jailynn Taylor describes Michelle Obama talking about how America wasn't ready to accept her natural hair. She assimilated, but now she's taking back control of her hair.

Wearing your Afro hair in any arena of the workplace opens a platform for all kinds of reviews. Therefore, deciding to wear my (Shelia's) natural hair to work especially during a time when there was less public tolerance for the natural look within a professional setting was a mental resolve for me. My mindset was, "This is me and how my hair grows, and I accept and like me."

When I got to work, I realized that my comfort with myself made others less comfortable with me. Some coworkers stopped and stared, mouths agape. More friendly ones asked,

"What did you do to your hair?" The bold ones asked to touch my hair!

I didn't stop wearing my natural hair. Soon, everyone got used to it and the hullabaloo simmered down to whispers and side glances. What other women besides those with Afro hair feel that their natural hair is on display at work? As a black woman, why must we ponder the effects our hair has on others in the workplace? It is an amazing phenomenon!

I concluded that my natural hair was a good thing, regardless of negativity, assumptions, or associations others make. My hair is good hair. God says human creation is "very good" in Genesis 1:31 and drops the mic! I'm part of human creation, so that declaration from my Creator is all I need to wear my natural hair at work or anywhere else.

Lord, I will go to work wearing my natural hair with the bold remembrance that you said it is very good!

16   When My Natural Hair Goes to Work with Me

It's time for us to stand up and be noticed. And it's time for us to reclaim our ancestral legacies. And it's time for us to realize that we are beautiful just the way that we are. Our features don't need to be slimmed down or photoshopped or smoothed. I think it's important for us to see ourselves as beautiful and strong and powerful and represented.

—Bisa Butler

If you were to open my (Sylvia's) bathroom cabinet on any given day, you'd find an assortment of flexi rods, perm rods, creams, butters, oils, and straight pens. It's like a mini store. All the items are a testament to how much money and time I've invested in styling my hair for the work week. Gone were the days of the simple twist out I wore in college. For work, I need natural hairstyles that can last me all week without requiring major touch-ups. If I'm not careful though, it can be easy to get lost in the opinions of others instead of what really matters, which is the health and beauty of my natural hair.

I used to wear a lot of protective hairstyles to work—updos with flat twists, Havana twists, faux buns, and extensions. It felt both freeing and limiting. Protective styles are convenient, but after a while, I missed my own natural hair. When I have my natural hair out, I know that I am being my true, authentic self. I am declaring that I am beautiful as I am without the fake curls or long weave. One thing I didn't miss though was the horror of coming into the ladies' room at work and looking in the mirror to find that the flexi rod set I had unrolled and shaped that morning in my mirror at home had gone completely askew. Flexi rods are just another styling tool, akin to rollers that can be used to create uniform curls that make kinky hair appear closer to someone with curly hair. In those moments, I'd wish I had a protective hairstyle instead so I wouldn't have to "fix" my hair.

What I slowly realized was that I wanted to live up to a false image of what I thought my hair *should* look like. If it was stretched out and fluffy, I worried it looked too big, shocking, or wild. If it shrunk down due to humidity, I worried that it looked too small or not dramatic enough. Would wearing my natural hair be seen as provocative? What was enough? What does enough look like?

When we choose to wear or not wear our natural hair to work based on what people think, we allow people's opinions to have too much power over us. Organizations have dress codes and company culture, but those should not dictate our hairstyles (though sometimes they do). Natural hair is not less professional than other hair textures. Whether or not to wear our natural hair at work means asking ourselves:

What natural hair style is in keeping with the company's culture?
What am I afraid of?
What does it matter anyway?

Imagine the worst scenario in your head of what could happen. Is a client's, colleague's, superior's, or subordinate's rejection at the center of it? If so, remember your confidence comes from within and plan a response for each set of reactors.

The times I've been the most afraid to wear a new style, and did it anyway, I was shocked at how much I had made a big deal out of nothing. People didn't make mean comments as I'd imagined and I even received a few unexpected compliments.

I promise myself I will wear my natural hair more at work—in any style I choose.

17 Age & Thinning Hair

So even to old age and gray hairs, O God, do not forsake me.

—*Psalm 71:18 NRSV*

"A person is either going to die young and pretty or old and ugly!" were my daddy's words to me one day out of the blue. "Yep, Shelia, a person is either going to die young and pretty or old and ugly!" Daddy went on to explain that as a person grew older, he or she was going to eventually lose such youthful characteristics as a built physique and head full of hair. His point was that no one will be able to hold on to good looks with age, so do not idolize the outward. Instead, accentuate the inner character.

Such mini random-but-wise conversations with my daddy, who lived his life as a man of valor, taught me that aging will affect my looks and eventually even my hair. I work out, am cognizant of eating healthily and taking vitamins, yet I see my hair graying, thinning on the crown of my head and along my hairline. I watch other women much older than me age gracefully with traces of distant, youthful beauty. When some try to hide their hair loss resulting from aging, I want to remind them that even when they are old and gray, God hasn't forsaken them. Their hair—its thinness and gray tendrils—is an honor.

It is significant for younger women to have the gray-haired women among them to learn how to age gracefully with dignity by accentuating their inner character as well as their hair with stylishness.

Know that the graying of your hair means God has given you an abundance of beauty within your heart. Choose to wear your hair with an elegance that reflects how gorgeous you still are and how you still have a God-given purpose to be a beautiful mirror for younger women to draw strength.

Dear Lord, I thank you for the graceful graying of my hair as I grow older.

18   God has already anointed my head.

You anoint my head with oil, my cup overflows.
—Psalm 23:5b NIV

Ancient shepherds most likely originated the practice of anointing. Lice and other insects often got into the wool of sheep, burrowing into the sheep's ears and killing the sheep. Shepherds would pour oil on the sheep's head to make the wool slippery, making it impossible for insects to get near the ears of the sheep. From this practice, anointing of oil became symbolic of protection, blessing, and service. People were anointed with oil to signify God's blessing or call on their lives to serve.[1]

My (Shelia) seasons of experimenting with different hair regimens were always due to my attempt to look like someone else or to impress others. My poor hair choices resulted in some damage to my hair growth.

It was during those times that I needed reminding that God had already anointed my head with oil—spiritual oil of protection, blessing, and service.

Dear God, I will be content with my hair.

19   The Black Hair Community

A woman who uses her sister as her hairdresser needs no mirror.

—*Akan Proverb*

Life is an endless struggle full of frustrations and challenges, but eventually you find a hairstylist you like.

—*Unknown*

I (Shelia) spent hours in hair salons getting my hair done during the era of the Jheri curl. I would go from a curl to a relaxer and then back again to a curl. Going back and forth between these two styles eventually damaged my hair and even permanently changed the texture and porosity of my hair.

At these salons, I met countless beauticians, from experienced stylists who loved their work to novices who were not yet well-established but tried hard to impress. But rarely did those who worked on my hair fully demonstrate an understanding of my natural hair. When the natural hair moment resurfaced in the 2000s and became the "new" look for African-American women, I was excited to find a black beautician in my community who knew how to work with my natural hair. Her name was Ms. P. She knew how to keep my natural hair texture and length by using the best products for my hair and trimming my split ends in a way that stimulated my hair growth. I would also meet other talented beauticians and hair stylists—my hair sistahs—who cared for my natural hair like miracle workers. Their fingers made my hair come alive.

In early West African societies, the hairdresser occupied an elevated position in society. It was believed that a person's hair contained her spirit, so the one who took care of it within the community had to be skilled *and* trustworthy.[1] Today, in the black community, let's celebrate and support our trained, talented, and trusted natural hair stylists and beauticians who understand the history, diversity, and intricacies of black hair—its curl patterns and porosity levels, the effects of products on our hair texture and scalp—and who know how to do creative styles with the versatile textures of black hair.

I applaud all the natural hair stylists who care for our hair as if it was their own. I will find a hairstylist for my natural hair who is skilled and knowledgeable.

20 Heavy Hair

There was not a man so highly praised for his handsome appearance as Absalom . . . Whenever he cut the hair of his head—he used to cut his hair once a year because it became too heavy for him—he would weigh it, and its weight was two hundred shekels by the royal standard.
—2 Samuel 14:25–26 NIV

Heavy hair is what I (Shelia) see on media and labels of hair products. The thickness, fullness, and voluminosity are what I covet for my hair. I sometimes wrestle with myself, wondering why.

The Bible character Absalom had such heavy hair that whenever he cut his hair, the shorn locks weighed five pounds (2 Samuel 14:26 NLT)! The mention of Absalom's long, heavy hair, however, prefaces the story of his uprising against his father, King David. Absalom's hair indicated his vanity and pride in his looks, which he used to steal the people's love from the king. Absalom then went to battle to take the kingdom, and during that conflict, in the forest of Ephraim, while riding on his mule, his hair got caught in the branches of a large tree. Absalom was left dangling in midair while the mule he was riding kept on going. An adversary found Absalom hanging in the tree by his heavy hair and killed him.

The story makes me ask myself: Do I want heavy hair out of vanity?

Lord, the coil pattern and fullness of my natural hair was heavenly created by you for me. I will be glad and rejoice in how you have made me and the hair you have given me.

21 *My Wake Moment*

> *"There's such a freedom that comes with loving yourself, accepting who you are and embracing your purpose. We live in a world where there is constant pressure to compete and compare. However, there is a place spiritually and a space mentally where all of the pressures cease. There is a place where the validation of man can't compete with the realization of self-worth! I am happy with the ME God created me to be. I've not always been here, but I'm so glad I made it!"*
> *—Tasha Cobbs Leonard*

The Word asks how can you say you love God, whom you've never seen, and then hate the brother or sister, whom you see every day? The same question applies to loving yourself. How can you say you love God and hate your own hair that the awesome Lord gave you?

There are times when I (Shelia) get up in the morning, remove my silk scarf, look at my hair, sigh, and think: "It's going to take a minute with this mess!" Then I remember God's love for my natural hair and that it is a gift. So instead, I ask myself, "How can I be wowed by my hair?"

> *Thank you, Lord, for another day! I love the skin I am in. I love the hair I have. You said in Psalms 139:14 that I am created wondrously by you so I know that applies to my hair, its texture coiled to your prescribed desire. My hair is intentionally me. No accidents here. I am going to be kind to my hair and style it with grace and gentleness. I will praise you through a faith-filled day because my natural crown is set to reflect the beauty of me!*

22   Know Thy Hair

Who taught you to hate the texture of your hair? . . . You should ask yourself who taught you to hate being what God made you.

—Malcolm X

Malcolm X asked this question about our hair texture at a speech he gave in Los Angeles in 1962. The texture of Afro hair was seen as something to hate rather than to love. However, Song of Solomon, 6:3–5 AMP, speaks to the intimate love God has for us and how our coils reflect a healthy love. This is being wowed by our hair!

When we educate ourselves about our hair texture, we teach ourselves that our natural hair demonstrates the cherished love God has for us and that each strand of our hair is eclectic in appearance and in creativeness. We teach ourselves to love our hair and to focus on the health of our hair.

Healthy hair has ideal moisture absorption and retention capabilities, does not become dry easily, and has elasticity and sheen. This means it stays hydrated, bounces, and has luster. The idea that managing our hair is a chore or something to hate is a lie and ultimately detrimental to our self-esteem.

I commit to understanding my natural hair—its texture, porosity, and density. Each strand is uniquely me.

23   A Prayer for Children & Alopecia

Leave the little children alone, and don't try to keep them from coming to me, because the kingdom of heaven belongs to such as these.

—*Matthew 19:14 CSB*

The little girl in the grocery store smiles at me again. Her skin on her head is tight and smooth without any hair, save for a whisper of a curl at the nape of her neck. The little girl is definitely of school age. How old is she? I wonder as she and her mom push their cart past me down the dairy aisle. Four or five years old, I concluded when I overheard her bright, chirpy comment to her mother:

"That lady smiled at me!"
"That's because she thinks you're pretty!" her mother quickly said, loud enough for me to hear.

Children living with alopecia have parents living with a child with alopecia. Knowing your beautiful child's hair will never grow or that she is balding can become disheartening if you let it. The confident response of that mother in the grocery store was reflected in her daughter's image of herself. Her daughter felt beautiful because her mom saw her as beautiful.

If you are a parent of a child who has hair loss, there are intentional things you can do to help your child see themselves through the lens of beauty. I (Shelia) use affirmation statements with my adult daughter Melissa who has alopecia. We used to recite the statements together at the end of her day. I also made a mental list of positive descriptive words to put in front of her name whenever I would text her or FaceTime her. I began with "Gorgeous Melissa," "My Regal Daughter," or "Fabulous-looking Melissa." I also started emailing her daily hair prayers. Each hair prayer was linked to a promising verse of scripture. She really loved these.

Saying affirmation statements daily, posting positive statements in your child's lunch box or on the mirror in their bedroom, or regularly greeting your child with an extended name that highlights a positive message are all ways to incorporate meaningful interaction into your child's daily life.

Dear Lord, thank you for fully loving and accepting my child. Let her be full of wisdom and have a healthy self-image. You, who make all things work together for the good (Romans 8:28), equip her to live out an impactful destiny because of her alopecia, not in spite of it.

24 Black Hair in Church

We don't go natural; we return to natural. Natural, is where it began.

—Unknown

Christians of African descent can trace our history back two thousand years to the very first leaders in the early church. Tertullian of Tunisia, Athanasius of Alexandria, and Augustine of Algeria were African theologians in the early church. There is also a powerful black presence in the Bible such as: Phinehas, grandson of Aaron (the brother of Moses), whose name means "Nubian," who were a dark-skinned African people (Exodus 6:25); Moses's wife, who was a Cushite, who were a group of African people coming from the region south of Egypt and characterized by black skin (Numbers 12:1); Jethro, Moses's father-in-law, the priest of Midian; Zephaniah the prophet; Bathsheba, wife of David (Sheba is an African tribe); Ruth the Moabitess; and the Ethiopian eunuch, who served the Kandake, the "queen of the Ethiopians" (Acts 8:27 NIV).

Black Christian history began in Africa, not with slavery in America. But, during slavery in America, enslaved black women were forced to keep their hair covered all week. They often took off their scarves and did their hair for church on Sundays. Church was a special space, to be ourselves and feel proud about it. It was where black women traded information about their hair.[1] My mother's generation was known for wearing big church hats like they were heavenly crowns.

Doing both of my daughters' hair for church was a big deal, especially for Easter, which is my favorite holiday of the year.

Preparing for that Sunday morning meant more than ruffle-tipped bobby socks and pretty dresses; it meant beautiful hairstyles. Defined even parts. Rubber band pigtails and barrettes. Hair done Saturday night to emerge curly, cute, and Polaroid-ready the next morning.

Given this legacy, we wear our natural hair with pride as we identify with a tradition that is rooted both in faith and in history.

Thankful for the heritage I have of black Christians in the early church, I wear my hair with God-given pride, confidence, and satisfaction wherever I find myself, especially in the sanctuary.

25   The Labor of Hair Care

"There are times when I like to give a little edge, even when it comes to my hair. . . . I love having my own hair out, but I'm not afraid of switching up and trying something new."

—Naomi Raine

Hair follicles regularly need rejuvenation. It takes a labor of love for you to consistently give your hair and scalp what it needs to be healthy and grow. What is true in the spiritual realm is paralleled in the material realm: all lifelessness does not end in finality. Consistent hair and scalp care can, with time, reawaken hair follicles.

Learn about your hair. Ask: what type of hair do I have? Work with your hair to discover how it responds to nutrients and essential oils. Have fun seeing what natural hair styles flatter your face and fit your taste.

Be consistent, determined, and tenaciously focused on growing and maintaining your best natural hair. Abound in the work of the Lord, remember that God gave you your hair to care for and that your labor is not in vain.

I choose to become more consistent with my hair care and am determined to be self-disciplined to do what is right for my hair.

26 I surrender all.

*Then at the entrance to the tent of meeting, the Nazirite
must shave off the hair that symbolizes their dedication.
They are to take the hair and put it in the fire that is
under the sacrifice of the fellowship offering.*
— Numbers 6:18 NIV

In the Bible, we learn about a special group of men and
women whose hair was the symbol of their identity: the Nazirites. "Nazirite" is the English translation for the Hebrew word
nāzîr, meaning "separate" or "consecrated."[1]

Nazirites made a special vow to dedicate themselves to the
Lord by not drinking wine or beer and not cutting their hair.
The latter commitment was especially important because
allowing the hair to grow long on one's head was the sign of
his or her dedication to God.

When the time of their dedication had ended, Nazirites were
to shave off all their hair and sacrifice it as a burnt offering
to the Lord. It was for this very reason that Nazirites allowed
their hair to grow in the first place. The Nazirite vow was
unique in that the person who took it consecrated a physical part of him or herself to God instead of just a material
possession.[2] Nazirites fully dedicated themselves to the Lord,
from crown to foot, and their long, unshorn hair was both the
symbol of their dedication and the ultimate offering.

Can you imagine waiting for your hair to grow inch by inch,
coil by coil, month after month, only to shave off all your
visual glory and set it on fire? The Nazirite vow was one of
the most intimate of sacrifices a person could make. Though

an ancient practice, the Nazirite vow is a present reminder for me (Melissa) to dedicate how I live my life, and specifically how I treat my hair, to God. Letting my hair grow and being disciplined with how I wash, detangle, and moisturize it is a modern-day offering to the One who made my hair and its texture. When I care for my hair as much as God does, I am living in fellowship with my Creator.

Lord, let how I care for my natural hair be a form of worship.

27   Celebrate My Hair

I love changing styles, but if left up to me I wouldn't relax my hair. I would wear twists, braids, and cornrows forever. I really feel best when my hair is natural.

—*Brandy*

My (Shelia's) friend who teaches high school always styled her natural hair differently almost every week. She had a tight curl pattern texture to her lengthy Afro hair, which took whatever shape she desired to showcase it in. She could do curls or Bantu knots, big puff balls or chunky braids, or whatever she wanted. She shared with me that one day several of her black female tenth-grade students came to school with their hair natural and in a similar style as hers. One of them told my friend that she liked her hair. To get this compliment from a high school student was a big thing.

However, it wasn't until another random black woman at the grocery store told her that she really liked her hair and then began to ask about the style did my friend realize how good that spontaneous compliment made her feel. She had been celebrated by another black sister.

In Zephaniah 3:14–17, God talks about a celebration. The Lord God rejoices over us as a child of God. The rejoicing of our heavenly Lord is a jubilant gladness like banners flying over our heads and music playing with a loud shout of joyous singing. God quiets all doubts and naysayers with love. This declaration is clearly stated as the Lord exults over us with loud singing. It's a celebration of you! It's a celebration of me!

God not only desires our praise but also rejoices over us as children. This outpouring of jubilation over us lifts us and makes us want to embrace our beauty. Likewise, we should celebrate the beautiful natural hair of each other. Lift a sister up. Tell her that her coils rock! Say how gorgeous those locks or braids are and that those Bantu knots sit like a crown of glory on her head. Compliment your sister-friend today and let her know her natural hair is a wonderful song of elegance.

Dear God, thank you for all my sisters who are wearing their beautiful natural hair with pride.

28   Hair Hate

What's wrong with my hair? I just made history and people are focused on my hair? You might as well stop talking about it.

—*Gabrielle Douglas*

While I (Sylvia) wish it was different, working daily in the competitive workforce allows for quite a number of opportunities to respond properly to haters. There are haters all around. People who hate the way others look, how they wear their hair, or how they project their image or persona or performance. But what happens when that hater is yourself?

Just today, I found myself taking a break from doing some work in order to read an online editorial about an actress, view the photos, and gawk at the outrageous prices for the clothes mentioned in the captions. As women, we all have found ourselves being drawn to the glamour of another person's beauty or seemingly perfect life. What was meant to be a quick break can easily become an hour pouring over picture spreads and pining after the latest looks or even "lifestyles."

Hair haters are the worst because of the vanity in using hair to compare or compete. There have been movies made about the "big hair" image and how this helps one to gain momentum in their job or in their status or position. It can become very uncomfortable and even cruel if you are at the blunt end of the one being hated on because of your hair, whether your hair is thick or thin, big or a teeny-weeny 'Fro.

Natural hair haters thrive on misconceptions. There are myths that our hair is unmanageable, dirty, or not presentable unless it is straight. The scary thing is that sometimes those natural hair haters can be ourselves. We are out of touch with our own roots. Under wigs and weaves, we create a facade that is not only accepted by general society but is also secretly what we believe we need to do in order to look "polished."

The fact of the matter is, sometimes you are the hater and sometimes other people are hating on you and *your* natural hair. While flipping through those glossy sheets or scanning magazines online, if you ever find yourself thinking, "Gosh, if only I could be like her! Or look like that. Or have that straight, loose hair texture," you may have a problem.

Remember, only you are responsible for how you respond to your haters whether or not that hater is someone else or yourself. Acknowledge your own imperfections. When you admit to God your own pride and foolish choices, this helps you to grow in the security of who you are because you know that, as God's child, you please him with how your hair looks. Therefore, you can go to work or be in public and wear your hair, reigning with the potential to be your best self and a beautiful blessing to others.

Your response to your hair haters will bring glory and not shame, inspiration and not emptiness. Your positive response will help others who may struggle with hair haters to embrace their God-given beauty in worship and praise. God's everlasting love for you should be the standard by how you treat others. Live up to this great potential and wear your hair with security; don't let your hair wear you.

> *Dear God, I know that I encounter people who don't like my hair. I also know that I have compared my hair to others. Help me to love my hair.*

29 Touch—The Love Language of My Hair

She began to wet his feet with her tears, and she wiped them with the hair of her head and began kissing his feet and anointing them with the perfume.

—Luke 7:38 NASB

When was the last time you loved on your hair? Loving on your hair means having the mindset of using positive hair language. When you think of your hair, use language that demonstrates your love for your hair. Historically and still to this day, there has been too much hate language about our Afro hair; such pejoratives or slurs leave a hollow disregard for our hair in the minds of others, but especially in our mind. It's time to change the narrative and start afresh. It's time to replace the hate language of "tough, nappy, uncontrollable, hard, dry" with the love language of "textured, versatile, eclectic, full of body, shapely, natural, earthly, and queenly."

The Bible doesn't specify the length or texture of the hair of the woman of Bethany, but it does show that she recognized the life-giving comfort of her hair and provides beautiful imagery of what she did with her hair. After breaking open an alabaster flask of expensive perfume (Mark 14:3 ESV) and pouring it on Jesus's feet, she then cleaned them with her hair and her tears. There is no hate hair language in this story of pouring perfume from an alabaster jar onto Jesus's feet, wetting his feet with her tears, and wiping them with her hair. Only the language of worship and her deep understanding of his acceptance of her—even to the touching of her hair.

If you've heard hate words about your hair, words that seared a memory in your mind of the time, place, and emotions you felt, create a new memory now. See wearing your natural hair as an act of worship. Connect with this woman who wiped her tears off Jesus's feet using her hair. Begin to worship God by embracing love language about your hair.

Wonderful and awesome God, please help me to say positive words about my hair to honor you.

30 Small Hair Prayers

Now Jabez called on the God of Israel, saying, "Oh that You would bless me indeed and enlarge my border, and that Your hand might be with me, and that You would keep me from harm that it may not pain me!" And God granted him what he requested.

—1 Chronicles 4:10 ESV

The prayer of Jabez is a popular passage in the Bible. It is a small prayer of sincerity inserted within a lengthy genealogical list of the descendants of Judah. Praying about your hair may seem like a small prayer, but small prayers are whispers heard by God. Just like Jabez, who carried with him a name that meant "he causes pain," you may carry within you pains about your hair. It can be the pain of your hair not growing longer or thicker due to repeated chemical processing or your hair breaking off due to a hairstyle.

Whatever pain you carry, expect a big response from God as he listens to your small prayer about your hair. Small prayers give hope. Small prayers interrupt doubt. Small prayers are heard by your Creator, who knows your desires for your hair.

Hear, dear God, this simple small prayer about my hair.

31 *My hair is a member.*

> *"Why was it that I was so attached to straight hair, that I was continuing to damage myself to get it? What was it that was so important to me about having my hair straight that I was willing to forgo my actual health to maintain this standard that had been called beautiful? What's wrong with my view of my intrinsic beauty and value that I am willing to do that?"*
>
> —*Priscilla Shirer*

Thinking of my (Shelia) natural hair as the least important "member" of my body makes me treat my hair as a postscript to everything else. It then becomes easy to cover up, easy to procrastinate taking care of, and easy to hide it beneath something. But God did not make one part of me to be less precious than the other parts of my body. My hair is a member with its own place of significance and function.

The importance of my hair to the rest of my body parallels my importance in the body of Christ. I now practice glorifying God even in my hair care as I expect great things to come to God's people through what God does in and through me. My natural hair wasn't an afterthought to God. Even unto the tips of my coils, my Creator will do great work through me.

I now pledge to treat my hair with the same value as I would any other part of my body.

32   Scarves & Wigs

Your adornment must not be merely external braiding the hair, and wearing gold jewelry, or putting on dresses; but let it be the hidden person of the heart, with the imperishable quality of a gentle and quiet spirit, which is precious in the sight of God.

—*1 Peter 3:3–4 NASB*

Let me (Shelia) share a testimonial with you about a young lady I worked with named Denice who struggled with her hair image. Denice worked in the office of our school and each day cordially greeted the public wearing beautiful scarves and expensive wigs. She looked gorgeous in them. One day, I complimented her on a stylish head wrap. She told me, "I wear wraps and wigs to hide alopecia and thinning edges." She shared with a couple of us at work that she struggled with not feeling good about her appearance. We all responded by complimenting her on how well she served the public, always with a smile. We mentioned she was the first face everyone saw when entering the building and reflected genuine beauty, beauty from the heart. We celebrated her exuberant character.

Eventually, she came to work wearing a teeny-tiny, lovely shaped Afro with the sides and edges of her head closely shaved. She had discovered her beauty within.

She allowed her scalp to breathe. She religiously followed her hair regimen. Over time, her hair grew a lot. But neither scarves nor wigs nor more hair were substitutes for her loveliness. Outward adornment was not the essence of her beauty. She worked on her outward appearance and cared for her hair, but the substance of her beauty was her inner self, the unfading beauty of "a gentle and quiet spirit."

> *God, as you help me care for my hair, please daily help me to adorn my inner beauty. I will think of beauty as starting within.*

33   Fairytale Hair

I say, 'You gotta wear your hair exactly the way it is. You can be Wonder Woman, but you gotta be Wonder Woman with your hair. You can be Elsa, but you gotta be Elsa with your hair.

—*Viola Davis*

From folk tales to fairy tales to beauty pageants, our natural Afro hair is seldom seen as the standard of beauty. It is rare to find Afro hair in fairy tales as the hair the crown is placed on and the hair the prince kisses. Hence, it was a historic moment in 2019 to see four black women simultaneously hold the top prize in the major beauty pageants: Kaliegh Garris, Miss Teen USA; Nia Franklin, Miss America; Cheslie Kryst, Miss USA; and Zozibini Tunzi, Miss Universe. It takes courage for black women to enter beauty contests.

"I grew up in a world where a woman who looks like me, with my kind of skin and my kind of hair, was never considered beautiful," Tunzi said. "I want children to look at me and see my face. And I want them to see their faces reflected in mine."

The narrative is being rewritten as we begin to see black hair crowned in beauty pageants *and* also children's books display black princesses with natural hair. Books such as *Princess Grace* by Mary Hoffman; *I'm A Pretty Princess* by Crystal Swain-Bates; *Princess Hair* by Sharee Miller and *More Than A Princess* by Delanda Coleman and Terrence Coleman.

Lord, I thank you for displaying the beauty of natural Afro hair like mine and making my hair the crown of glory it is.

34 Princess Hair

"Rapunzel, Rapunzel, Let down your hair to me."
Rapunzel had magnificent long hair, fine as spun gold,
and when she heard the voice of the enchantress she unfas-
tened her braided tresses, wound them round one of the
hooks of the window above, and then the hair fell twenty
yards down, and the enchantress climbed up by it.
                          —Rapunzel *by The Grimm Brothers*

Incorporating my locs into the [character Ariel's] red
hair was something that was really special to me.
                                          —*Halle Bailey*

No offense to *Tangled*, Disney's version of the classic Grimm
fairy tale *Rapunzel*, but long blonde hair is never going to
grow naturally out of my (Sylvia's) head. Does that mean I'm
not qualified to get my prince?

Have you noticed that most of the hair featured in fairy tales
is long and straight? The only princess with short hair is Snow
White and the only princess with curly hair is Merida from
Brave. Even Tatiana from *Princess Frog* has straight, black hair
that's been curled and styled in a bun.

When Disney announced a live-action film version of *The
Little Mermaid* it was revealed that a black actress had been
cast for the title role of Ariel. After the trailer dropped, videos
surfaced online of young black girls' reactions. Ariel, who in
the animation is illustrated as a buoyant redhead, is shown
instead as an African-American woman with reddish-brown
locs.

Cameras caught little girls showing expressions of shock, crying, and smiling as a woman who looked like them sang the Disney classic, "Part of Your World."

Representation matters because when we see ourselves elevated, we are uplifted.

> *My natural hair is fairytale hair. It's magical, wonderful, and totally unique. I don't wish it any other way. I am the princess of my story and I won't let anyone tell me not to wear my natural hair styles in all their glory.*

35   Weakness

Whenever something went wrong when I was young—if I had a pimple or if my hair broke—my mom would say, "Sister mine, I'm going to make you some soup." And I really thought the soup would make my pimple go away or my hair stronger.

—Maya Angelou

I (Shelia) used to try some of the most outlandish things that the old folks would suggest trying, what we may call today old wives' tales. Like Maya Angelou thought her mom's soup was the cure for getting strong hair, I would believe whatever my elders told me about helping my hair grow. One such suggestion that I tried was taking pieces of my broken hair and burning them on the stove. At the time, we had a gas stove and I truly believed that burning the broken strands would somehow help make my hair stronger. Another hair-growing idea I tried when I was a little girl was having my hair plaited in tiny braids all over my head, after which small rubber bands were wound around each braid in the hope of stretching the hair out of the scalp to increase the length. Another favorite was catching rainwater in a bucket and then washing my hair in it. This was supposed to make it stronger and not break so easily, especially the edges. This all sounds ridiculous now, but having weak and broken areas of hair remains an issue.

As we focus on weak hair, think of how God wants us to address weaknesses. Give hair weaknesses the same attention God instructs us to give the weak areas of our lives. God does not want us to look away from our weaknesses but in humility to identify them, address them, and not to cover them up. Let's strive after God's way of doing things, even regarding our hair.

I will be honest and open with the Lord about what needs to be strengthened in my life, including my hair.

36 *I didn't marry your hair.*

> *I can't believe how hard they make it in society for black women to love their natural self—people of other races will be washing their faces and just leave the house, but God forbid a black girl does the same thing!*
> —Lipglossssssssss, TikTok Creator

Most men love hair on women.

My husband and I (Shelia) have been married for forty years and within those years he has seen my hair go through a plethora of metamorphoses. He has seen it in the Jheri curl, in a relaxer, in a hot comb press, in braided styles, and with weave in and out. He has seen it in teeny-weeny Afros to big fat hair blow-outs. He has seen a multitude of colors from jet black to many shades of browns, reds, and blondes. He has seen me order online hair rollers, tooth combs wide and skinny. He has seen me purchase all kinds of shea butter brands and curl sprays and coconut oils and hair oils at high-end to low-end prices. He has seen me in scarves and beads and hair clips, flowers, and bows. He has seen my hair frame and even shame my face with my parade of hair styles.

It never dawned on me how strong an opinion he had about my hair and how my hairdo choices made him feel, until one day, years into our marriage, he finally said to me, "I don't know why you're always messing with your hair. I didn't marry your hair. I just like it natural. That's my favorite way! I LOVE," he reiterated "your hair in a natural Afro style."

This made me realize that I had all along what he liked, although I still wear braids, which he hates. I wear them because it gives my hair a chance to rest from constant manipulation, and the braiding helps my hair to grow.

I have met and talked to other women who experienced the same thing. One young bride who has alopecia recounted to me when she had to tell her then fiancé that the wigs she'd been wearing were not her real hair and that she had alopecia. She was relieved when he said to her, "You are much more to me than hair. I love you for you."

Dear Lord, please remind me in my down moments that I am more than just my hair to the one who loves me.

37 *He loves my hair, he loves it not.*

> *Pilate put her hand on Hagar's head and trailed her fingers through her granddaughter's soft damp wool . . . "It's the same hair that grows out his own armpits. The same hair that crawls up out of his crotch in up his stomach. All over his chest. The very same. It grows out of his nose, over his lips, and if he ever lost his razor it would grow all over his face. It's all over his head, Hagar. He got to love it."*
>
> —*Toni Morrison*, Song of Solomon

There is a continual tug of war of pain in my (Shelia's) mind because I see so many black men who don't love our hair. The quote of the character Pilate in Toni Morrison's *Song of Solomon* is often not what's communicated to me and this hurts.

I have often walked into a coffee shop with my fabulous 'Fro shooting upward and turned heads of white men, but rarely black men. I've received compliments from white men on my coils in the grocery store, but seldomly from a black man.

The media shouts a load of approval from black men for black women's hair that is long and straight, characteristic of nonblack women.

My eldest daughter has helped me with this hair hurt from black men. "Mom, when you build up yourself, you give others the freedom to build you up too," she told me. I love this profound thought.

When we showcase our natural hair with confidence and self-awareness, black men can love the unique beauty of our hair.

When I love my natural hair, it gives others the freedom to love my natural hair and makes me enjoy wearing it whether others—even black men—see its beauty or not.

38 *Grief & Alopecia*

*Truly, truly, I say to you, that you will weep and mourn,
but the world will rejoice; you will grieve, but your grief
will be turned into joy!*

—*John 16:20 NASB*

Grief can lead to alopecia. A young lady I met at a memorial
service talked incessantly, but she was always smiling. I did not
know her but knew all too well the stages of grieving (denial,
anger, bargaining, depression, acceptance) and I could tell she
was grieving.[1] She shared with me picture after picture of herself
with different hairstyles. Along with each picture was a story of
how she created the style. In all the pictures, she had beautiful,
long, thick, coarse-looking hair falling to her shoulders.

But now her hair was a teeny-weeny 'Fro that looked damaged
and dry, thinning at the edges. She said her hair began falling
out during the journey of her loved one dying. Her grieving
was so traumatic that it brought on breakage and alopecia.

Grief is a universal stress that can inflict suffering on our
bodies including our hair. The stress of bereavement can accel-
erate alopecia.[2] Hair follicles could suffer because of a lack of
essential nutrients in our body during the grieving process
due to not eating properly.

Jesus understands our tears. This truth can be of help with
hair health and healing.

*Dear Jesus, help those who are in grief maintain emo-
tional stability and healthy habits.*

39   Consistency & Care

> *[Daniel] continued kneeling on his knees three times a day, praying and giving thanks before his God, as he had been doing previously.*
>
> —Daniel 6:10 NASB

Consistency takes having accountability. There are many times my daughter Sylvia acts as my accountability hair care partner. She reminds me and encourages me when it is my hair wash day. Whenever I keep my braids in too long, she will ask, "Mom, how long have you had your hair in that protective hairstyle? You know it's time to take those braids down."

Having an accountability partner helps me because it is so hard to stay consistent in hair care since I must be consistent in both process and product. Sometimes it seems like my hair has a mind all its own or that it's controlled by some force outside my body. I know this sounds ridiculous, but if you're like me, it's hard to get the same style exactly the same way each day. I have a ton of photos where one hairstyle looks different each time. And I often think the humidity may have a lot to do with it, but mainly it comes from not staying consistent with my hair regimen or with the products I am using.

When you have an accountability partner who you know is going to regularly check your routine, it helps you keep up a continuous pattern, which is what being consistent means. Daniel was one such example in the Bible. People could set their time dials by the consistency of Daniel because he regularly prayed three times a day every day. He never broke his pattern of prayer because prayer was relational for him. He was speaking to a miracle-working holy God who is Lord and whom he could base his life on.

The consistency of Daniel's prayer life was fueled by his relationship with God. Being consistent in your hair care should stem from your understanding of the depth of love and care God has for you. Your Creator doesn't want you to neglect or haphazardly care for the beautiful creation you were given. Your consistent care of your hair is a prompt for praise to God, who gloriously made you.

Dear God, help me to find an accountability hair care partner. I want to be consistent in my hair care because I recognize that being consistent is an act of obedience that reflects your character.

40 More than My Hair

I am not my hair. I am not my skin. I am the soul that lives within.

—India Arie

It is hard to see potential during barrenness. We feel alone in this empty space—this place of barrenness. How do we move forward with hope and expectancy? One way is to not just identify with our hair but to recognize our inward self. If your barren scalp never bears hair, then ask God what the plan for your baldness is.

God's answer might be to beautifully wear it with regality. God's purpose for your life is more than what's physically on your head. The decision you make about your baldness must be one that you feel pleases God. You are God's own hand-iwork (Ephesians 2:10, AMPC). The Creator is pleased with how carefully you are crafted and has a plan for your life, a destiny for you to walk in, and "good works" prearranged and made ready for you to live. God already knew about your form of barrenness, but because God loves you, be assured that you will always be pregnant with potential for a full life.

I have the inner spiritual strength to feel comfortable around others with my baldness. I choose to focus on my potential, who I am.

41   Divine Natural Hair

> *As I watched, Thrones were set up and the Ancient of
> Days took his throne. His clothing was white as snow,* the
> hair on his head like pure wool; *His throne was flames
> of fire, with wheels of burning fire.*
> >   —*Daniel 7:9 NABRE, emphasis added*

> *The hairs of his head were white, like white wool, like
> snow. . .*
> >   —*Revelation 1:14 ESV*

A ram in the bush (Genesis 22:13), a bush on fire (Exodus
3:2), a gentle whisper (1 Kings 19: 12 NIV)—God is revealed
through these things and more in the Bible. The ways God
appeared to people were specific and significant. God was very
much in the details. The Bible books of Daniel and Revela-
tion describe God's appearance. In both accounts, one detail
that is singled out is God's hair texture. It is likened to wool
or "pure wool." God had a head of thick, coarse, curly hair.
Imagine God enthroned in the heavens, hair radiating from
his head like an Afro-shaped cumulus cloud.

That God's hair is described in the Bible affirms hair as an
important feature of one's identity to our Creator. Hair is
important to God for it to be mentioned in the Bible, especially in connection to our Lord. That the Bible describes
God's hair as woolly affirms Afro-textured hair. The texture
of God's hair as wool or naturally curly, clearly denotes our
Creator's approval of our hair.

While tightly coiled natural hair isn't the standard of beauty in a society that prizes straight hair, the Bible's truth is that our hair is valued by God so much that God shares the same thick curls.

When you look at your natural hair in the mirror, or take those selfies with friends, know that your hair reflects the Divine.

I praise you, God, for affirming my natural hair texture in scripture. When I'm tempted to compare my hair to straight hairstyles and find it wanting, please remind me that my Afro-textured hair reflects the Bible's description of your hair.

42 Just Like Eagles' Feathers

Nebuchadnezzar was forced to go away from people, and he began eating grass like an ox. He became wet from dew. His hair grew long like the feathers of an eagle, and his nails grew like the claws of a bird.

—*Daniel 4:33 NCV*

I (Shelia) have to watch out for feeling vain about my hair, especially when I get compliments on a new updo and I know I am looking good! Having healthy hair esteem becomes vanity when I feel like my hair is all about me and how good I look to other people.

King Nebuchadnezzar was vain and feared by many until God took away his throne and forced him to "live with the wild animals, away from people" for seven years (Daniel 4:32 CEV). Instead of the once proud king's head bearing a crown, his unkempt hair reflected his humbled state. After the seven years were up, God gave Nebuchadnezzar back his ability to rule. With fresh humility, Nebuchadnezzar praised God instead of himself.

We can feel vain about our hair or elaborate, expensive hairstyles. Yet, our hair can be gone tomorrow. Our hair can fall out when we grieve or get sick. We may not have the energy to take care of it during a difficult season of our lives. Life circumstances can come our way and rob us of good hair days. Let's have an attitude of thankfulness toward God for those good hair days and approach them with humility, praising God instead of ourselves for the beauty of our hair and the ability to style it. Let's take pride in how God made our hair, not in how impressive our hair makes us look to other people. Then, every day can be a good hair day.

> *Dear God, help me to not be vain about my hair. I want to feel proud about how I style my hair without needing to make comparisons to, or get compliments from, other people.*

43   The Aroma of My Hair

And walk in love, just as Christ also loved you and gave Himself up for us, an offering and a sacrifice to God as a fragrant aroma.

—*Ephesians 5:2 NASB*

A friend from Eritrea came to me one day and said she had something to share with me (Shelia). She told me that she was planning to have ten inches or more cut off her hair so she could give it to a charity that makes ethnic dolls. I could hear the passion in her voice as she talked about doing this. She wanted her hair to become a part of a bigger picture of sharing in the hopes and joys of bringing a smile to a child's face who could see herself in these dolls.

I wondered why she chose such a personal way of reaching out to this charity by actually having so much of her beautiful hair cut off. I asked her what brought her to this conclusion. She said that she felt that giving up something so close to her which God had given to her would be like an act of love, and so after much prayer, she decided to do it.

As believers, we are urged to be imitators of God as beloved children and to walk in love. This love is demonstrated as an act of total surrender like Jesus did as an offering in our place. The complete sacrificial atonement for our sins was a fragrant aroma to God.

You may not necessarily be led to cut your long hair as my friend did, but God is asking you to love and live completely knowing that all you have is God-given—including your hair. When we live as imitators of God, we get to experience a deeper appreciation of ourselves, our skin, our hair, and the overall making of who we are. This deep appreciation becomes a fragrant aroma to God.

Dear God, I want to embrace my hair as a gift from you and offer it back to you to honor and glorify you.

44   Counting My Hairs

Indeed, the very hairs of your head are all numbered.
—Luke 12:7 NIV

My mother, Madear, used to braid my hair. She would count the sections she parted my hair in. Usually about eight sections. Two side ponytails. One big one hanging over my forehead. Another big braid that gathered the crown section of my head and then four mid-size plaits in the back that were connected together. Sometimes she would tie a ribbon on each braid's tip to add a little something. When she was done braiding, I always felt so happy and pretty.

As I look back on it now, it wasn't so much because of the style that I felt special but rather because of the value-added time she took. Counting something means taking time to attribute attention to each individual piece. The Most High God pays such attention to us; to all the diverse hair textures of our Afro hair with our variations of patterns, sizes, densities, strand diameters, and feel. God counts each strand of our curl pattern. Our Creator's value placed on each of us can never be discounted because others look negatively at our hair.

I recognize the intimate value, Lord, you have placed on me because you know me—even to the numbers of hair on my head.

45 Natural Hair in Hospitals

Don't remove the kinks from your hair, remove them from your brain.

—*Marcus Garvey*

We were always so excited as a family whenever it was family vacation time because this meant road trip time! We'd pack up all the kids' favorite snacks and favorite toy or game that would keep each of them occupied for hours and from asking, "Are we there yet?" and we hit the road at the break of dawn. One particular vacation, we decided to rent a large van that seated eight because everyone would have more room for stuff. One of our daughters, who was three years old at the time, took her favorite doll, and when we arrived at our destination, we couldn't find it. It was stuck under a seat. In my effort to retrieve the little doll, I hadn't noticed my daughter behind me and in just a split second she fell out of the van and hit her head on the pavement. We realized that a tiny stone had lodged itself in her soft scalp between her rows of cornrows. We rushed her to a hospital.

The first thing the nurse said to me was, "We can't see anything until you take out the braids."

I could easily see the stone. I asked, "What do you mean take out the braids?"

They told me they would not begin any procedure until I took down every single braid! I had braided my daughter's hair in rows of braids with colored beads on the ends. It took a while to unloose them and all the while my daughter was crying from the pain of the fall. And I was worried about the tiny pebble lodged in her scalp. I knew the hospital staff's discomfort with my daughter's hair was why we were told to conform to what was comfortable for *them* before they could help her. I felt the sting of annoyance of conformity.

Having to conform our hair to what is acceptable or comfortable for others is played out in many other situations. It is society's way of saying, "You're not okay the way you are, so change it." But Romans 12:2 (KJV) reads: "Do not be conformed to this world, but be transformed by the renewing of your mind. . ."

I commit myself to thinking only the best about my hair, so I don't feel I must conform.

46 Image Builders

I was going through this identity transformation and hair was very much a part of that.

—A'Lelia Bundles

There are so many transformative image builders in our history who have left a legacy for black women. An image builder in my (Shelia's) life was my fifth-grade teacher Mrs. Pitts. I loved it when Mrs. Pitts would call me to her desk, take a few dollars out of her purse, and send me to the cafeteria to buy her lunch. Running this errand for her gave me the chance to eat my lunch in the classroom with her. I watched as she turned her head side to side while she ate and graded papers. I loved looking at her hair, especially in her profile view. Mrs. Pitts styled her totally natural hair in a puffed-up giant roll bun swooped along the back of her head with some of her hair cropped evenly across her forehead and brushed back to join the bun. She always wore a regal hair clamp pin to the side of her bun. Her entire image spelled queenliness to me. She would always say to me with a smile, "You're going to be a wonderful writer someday." I relished her words. When I got to high school, I wore my hair exactly like Mrs. Pitts.

God has chosen our image to be that of royalty (1 Peter 2:9 NIV) and our identity transformation means having a life's purpose. It is now time for us to be image builders for black women and girls in our sphere of influence as we style our natural hair. And to be a reminder of the regality, strength, confidence, courage, and power that lies within all of us who are black women!

I accept the responsibility to be an image builder by wearing my hair natural.

47   Don't be a long hair hater.

> *"I'm telling you my hair story, but you realize this ain't just about hair. This is the thing God used for me to help me begin to see clearly the areas of my life where I lacked a sense of significance that was rooted in Him, a sense of beauty because of the beauty He's given me, the intrinsic value that He's invested in me. That I don't have to look like her."*
>
> —*Priscilla Shirer*

There were countless times during my (Shelia's) early college dorm days that I would be in the restroom in front of the mirror fixing my hair when one of the white girls on the floor would come out of the shower with towels wrapped around her body and hair, then take the towel off her head and fling her long wet hair; flipping droplets of water in my area. It made me irate. I felt this way again sitting in the beauty salon waiting my turn and watching my beautician comb through the long hair of another black woman, prepping her hair for an elaborate braid style that my beautician would eventually create with another salon hairdresser, the two of them together braiding the long hair of the patient patron. Agitation and jealousy were what I felt as I looked at her long, thick natural hair billowing out over her arms.

Women with long hair can evoke hate when I wish my own Afro hair would just grow an inch more! I divert my eyes from the temptation of envy as I look at the long, gorgeous hair of others—Afro and straight. I don't want to be a long hair hater.

There is nothing wrong with having long hair or wanting to grow longer hair. It becomes an issue when you are willing to "do whatever it takes" to have long hair, when it becomes an obsession, especially if your motivation is to appease current beauty standards.

The context of 1 Corinthians 11:15 is wearing head coverings when praying or prophesying as was the cultural practice back then.[1] Paul's emphasis on long hair as a woman's glory highlights the cultural practice of covering the head for the sake of modesty. The principle still holds true that if a woman has long hair, it is a glory to her and should reflect her relationship with her Lord.

To all my sistas who have long hair, wear your voluminous cloud of beauty without apologies but use it as a bridge to be kind.

To my sistas who gaze upon the long hair of other women, don't propagate hair hate but instead connect with your own hair glory. Instead of focusing on growing your hair longer, make sure your hair—whatever its length—is the healthiest it can be.

Dear Magnificent God, thank you that my natural Afro hair is a glory to me and thank you for all my sistas' hair lengths that show the vastness of your creativity.

48   Educate the next generation.

I leave you, finally, a responsibility to our young people.
The world around us really belongs to youth, for youth
will take over its future management.

                                    —*Mary McLeod Bethune*

When my daughter was in third grade, she had to do a
report for school. She had a hard choice between Sojourner
Truth or Phillis Wheatley. Both were powerful black women.
Sojourner Truth was born into slavery in New York in 1797
and after gaining her freedom in 1827, she became a well-
known anti-slavery speaker, famous for her speech "Ain't I a
Woman?" About forty-four years earlier, Phillis Wheatley was
born around 1753 on the west coast of Africa, kidnapped by
slave traders, and brought to America in 1761. She became the
first African American to publish a book of poems.

My daughter diligently studied both women and ended up
deciding on Sojourner Truth because she loved the way the
title of her famous speech sounded. And since a requirement
for my daughter's school report was to present before her class
speaking in first person voice, this gave her a chance to enjoy
reciting some of the speech.

My daughter also wanted to dress like Sojourner Truth
during the presentation and wear her hair like Sojourner, but
we couldn't find a picture showing Sojourner Truth's hair. All
the pictures we saw of both women—Phillis Wheatley and
Sojourner Truth—showed their hair covered by a bonnet.

Black women's hair was hidden in slavery and throughout much of history, but our voice and mind could not be

hidden. It was the persistent, scholarly intelligence and bold, creative determination of black women like Sojourner Truth and Phillis Wheatley that prepared the way for the now-generation.

Born in 1875, Mary Jane McLeod Bethune had the right perspective when she wrote her last will and testament, leaving behind a legacy of educating youth. Let's be students of our hair and learn all about our hair within our history so that we can impact the young black women around us to learn about their hair and its divine testimonial—created by a holy God who formed its beauty.

I will study my hair and its history and use my knowledge to educate younger people so they will love and learn to care for their natural hair.

49   Self-Conscious about My Hair

*I would say that hair is a woman's glory and that you
share that glory with your family. And they get to see you
braiding it and they get to see you washing it . . . But it
is not a bad thing or a good thing, it's hair.*

—Maya Angelou

As I (Shelia) prepared for my work week, I would always think
ahead about how I would maneuver my natural hair into manageable styles that "fit" my workplace. How is the weather
today going to affect my hairstyle? What will the air moisture do to it today? How does this style frame my face? Can
I keep this style for at least a couple of days? How much prep
time is needed the night before for this style? Or can I make
it a quick, easy do to just put up in the morning? Oh no,
what about showering with this style? If I tie it up, will it still
look fresh? How will this style look with a casual dress or a
more professional dress? What to wear to highlight this style?
What jewelry? What colors? Does my natural hair shout out
too loudly? Am I over the top? How will I be received when
I wear my natural hair? I noticed one coworker staring at my
hair when I last wore this style—should I not wear it again?

Now I realize that I am overly self-conscious about my
natural hair at work. I am tired of overthinking how to
wear my natural hair. As Maya Angelou says, "It is not a bad
thing or a good thing—it's hair." God refers to my hair as
my ornament and glory (I Corinthians 11:15 AMP). One of
the definitions of the word *ornament* is "something that lends

grace, beauty, or festivity." My natural hair is a quality that adorns. My natural hair lends grace and beauty to my person.

I only need to wear it in a way that pleases me, makes me feel good about myself.

Dear God, my natural hair is my beautiful accessory given to me by you. I wear it boldly in my workplace in praise of you, who has wonderfully made me.

50   Protection is perfection.

Not a hair from the head of any of you will perish.
                                                    —Acts 27:34 NASB

According to the 2021 Dove Crown Research Study for Girls, hair bias and discrimination can start as early as five years old.[1] This systematic and structural racism, discrimination, and self-hate affects black children's social, emotional, and academic learning, leaving them feeling unprotected and vulnerable. Hair bias has a huge bearing on how they see themselves in the world.

Protecting the beauty narrative of Afro hair means we must find a safe space for the narrative about black natural hair in politics, social, educational, and commercial settings; and personally.

In Acts chapter 27, Paul was on a boat with a number of other prisoners on his way to Rome. A fierce storm struck and it seemed certain that the ship would sink and all on board would drown. Paul believed otherwise. God had assured him that, although the ship would be lost, all on board would be saved and Paul himself would eventually reach Rome. The phrase "for there shall not a hair fall from the head of any of you" is a proverbial phrase, an expression meaning the utmost safety or safe place. Paul wanted to assure all on board that they would be safe from momentous calamity because our sovereign God is the ultimate protector.

Verbal and attitudinal attacks on our hair can leave us emotionally shipwrecked. Let's not allow it to cause us to lose focus on the truth that our awesome God is our protector, guarding even our feelings. In our Creator's intentional will, our hair was made with perfection. God is our safe space. Knowing our Lord magnifies our beauty—in our hair—assures us that we are not shipwrecked by other people's biases about our hair. God's view of our hair offers us protection. In God's sight, our natural hair is perfect.

Thank you, God, for your protective plan and lead me to a safe mental and emotional state so I feel secure wearing my hair natural.

51   *It is well*

> *"I think well-being is so important for your spirit, soul,
> and body. Prayer and meditation for the spirit. Having
> faith keeps me well inside."*
>
> —*Cece Winans*

Getting my "hair done," as I (Shelia) grew up calling it, has
been a part of my life since early childhood. From sitting on
the floor in between my Madear's legs to sitting in salon chairs
or at a friend's kitchen table, I recall vivid memories of an intimate time of grooming and warm, socially interconnecting
that always made me feel wholly content.

The entire event of hair grooming is seen historically in
every African culture. Hair was always carefully groomed and
artistically crafted by talented individuals who understood
aesthetic standards and realized hair grooming was a significant part of community life.

I John 3:2 is saying that, as God's children, we are being
groomed and fashioned into a distinctive and unique design
and pleasing to our heavenly Savior. It is yet to be seen and
even beyond our imaginations what we'll finally become.

As we get our natural hair combed and picked out and
styled—"done"—know that as children of God, we are called
beloved by our Lord and our ultimate goal is to become like
the one who is spiritually grooming us for perfect wellness to
reflect our Creator and become like our Lord.

> *Thank you, God, for making me more like you today and
> reassuring me that my hair-grooming experience can be
> a reminder that I am beloved, and it is well.*

52 What does age have to do with it?

Even when you are old, I will take care of you. Even when your hair has turned gray, I will take care of you. I made you and will take care of you. I will carry you, and I will save you.

—*Isaiah 46:4 ICB*

I (Shelia) paused sipping my cinnamon latte and glanced at the silhouette of my two sister-friends in the window before us. We are all in our wisdom years, but in this brief moment, the lovely reflection of our natural Afro hair looked like the shape of lyrical notes bouncing off the window. I smiled and thought of a familiar tune, "What's Love Got to Do with It," but instead, I asked myself, "What does age have to do with it?"

I answered my own question by looking at the uniqueness of each of our natural hair styles. Each style suggested the time and attention we each took with our hair. So, the answer to my question was, "Wearing natural Afro hair is ageless." Caring for our natural hair as we age and seeing the changes in the length, thickness, color, or loss of it is just as important to us as older black women as much as it was when we were younger.

One day while I was shopping at a beauty store, trying to find the right hair to use for my protective hairstyle, I passed by the wig section and saw this older black woman with smooth caramel skin and such gorgeous white natural hair. Her hair resembled angel wings to me. I stopped and told her how pretty her natural hair color was. She said, "Thank you, honey. I guess I don't need this wig, huh?"

I said, "Not at all."

Age does not deter us from wanting our hair to continue to grow, to have that sheen and bounce and length. We never give up on wanting our natural Afro hair to embrace all the definitions of healthiness and beauty.

God reminds us of this. God lets us know again and again that we are significantly designed by our loving Creator, including our gray hairs. God hears our concern for the health of our hair and age doesn't stop our God from taking care of us.

Lord, thank you for keeping me in your mind even as I am aging.

SALON CHAIR SESSIONS

Again, we have this misconception of what "good hair" is. Whether it is what we have seen on television or what we have heard others say, or even our own vain imagination, good hair is simply healthy hair!

—Zenobia Jackson, *The Secrets of Going Natural: The Ultimate Guide to Loving Your Natural Hair*

WHAT IS NATURAL?

Natural hair is the hair you're born with. It's your God-given, straight-from-the-womb hair. Completely unaltered, not straightened or styled. It is the hair that first took root and sprung from the crown of your head.

You know that feeling of needing a touch-up? That's your natural hair peeking through. Natural hair speaks to ancestral heritage. It shapes and binds you to the continent. And hair doesn't lie.

There are negative stigmas with natural hair perpetuated by society, like the pencil test commonly used in countries like South Africa, to divide the haves and the have-nots. If the pencil didn't slide through your hair, your hair was considered to be too kinky and of African origin.

But today, we, as African-American women, largely perpetuate our own standards for natural hair. Either hiding it or straightening it to "standards." And if we fail to adhere to unstated rules, we can be criticized harshly for it.

Remember Gabby Douglas, the decorated Olympic gold medalist? After becoming the first African American to win the women's all-around gymnastics title at the 2012 Olympics, she asked, "What's wrong with my hair? I just made history and people are focused on my hair? You might as well stop talking about it." Black women criticized that her hair wasn't "laid": her natural roots were showing, and somehow, in this day and age, that is a bad thing.

Some people ask to touch it or call it a mane. It's deemed as "wild," unmanageable. Like a creature needing to be tamed.

But there is so much beauty in natural hair in its purest form. It defies gravity or bounces. It is both fragile *and* strong.

So when we say "natural hair," we aren't talking about anything other than the hair you were born with. Period.

Hair Textures, Hair-Type Charts & "Texturism"

"Black people's hair is like fingerprints," said black hair care entrepreneur and inventor Willie L. Morrow in his book *400 Years Without a Comb.* "There are never two heads of hair exactly alike."[1] Our Afro hair is distinct in the world. No other racial group has this physical marker. Because it is so different, we can only understand the intrinsic value of our unique natural hair texture through the limitless creativity of God. Embracing our natural hair is thus an opportunity to connect with the God who made us. Such is the invitation of *My Divine Natural Hair.*

We're tired of the phrase "good hair." There is no such thing as "good hair." But we have to believe that not only in our minds but also in our hearts. We have to change the language around how we think and talk about our hair.

A person can have multiple textures of hair on her head. The issue with the conventional hair texture chart (see Figures 1 and 2) is that what started out as a way for women to get to know their hair better turned into an implicit competition as to who could make their hair the biggest, curliest, and longest. What should have been a knowledge tool turned into a measuring stick. And depending on where your hair fell, you didn't measure up. The hair scale is notorious for putting kinky hair at the bottom. Women are judged by the texture of their hair. This is called "texturism."

The problem with texturism is that it makes you think that something is wrong with your hair the way it is. This problem goes beyond the funny bad hair days on TV. Our hair is labeled by TV commercials, film, media, and even at home or schools as bad. Rough. Unmanageable. A hot mess. So, we tuck and fold and try to hide our real hair.

HAIR TYPES

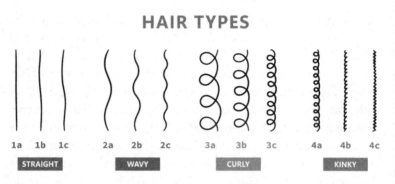

Figure 1. The conventional hair texture chart (Example 1).

HAIR TYPES

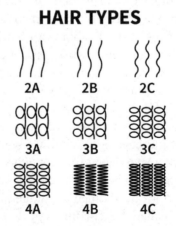

Figure 2. The conventional hair texture chart (Example 2).

Figure 3. Hair Checkup Cycle Chart © 2024 Sylvia Burlock.

But when does hiding our hair become hiding ourselves?

The three of us embrace our individual hair textures by using our hair checkup cycle chart (see Figure 3).

Our hair chart is set up differently than most because there isn't a scale from straight to kinky. Instead, it simply explains—in easy-to-understand language—your hair. Think of it as a checkup you get at the doctor. Our hair checkup focuses more on hair *health* than appearance. Hair texture is just one way of looking at your hair. Other characteristics to take into account are density and porosity. While density has to do with the thickness of your hair, porosity has to do with how the hair absorbs moisture. *Both* influence hair texture and how it can be styled and both need to be taken into account when considering your natural hair.

Different Journeys, One Story

On our hair checkup cycle chart, we replaced the usual A, B, and C classifications, which denote *grades* of hair, with "hot," "medium," and "mild" kinks. Who else is down for changing the way we look at our hair from a red letter your teacher would write on your homework to the degree of hotness you ask for when you order your Thai food?

We (Shelia, Melissa, and Sylvia) come from three different hair journeys and our hair reflects that. What makes our journeys the same is that we are kinky-haired women. At the same time, our hair thrives on versatility. This is why the hair checkup cycle chart doesn't put natural hair in a box or at the end of a scale. Take us for example:

> **Shelia** would say that her hair is 4b on the conventional scale. But on our hair checkup cycle, she is kinky medium. In other words, her hair is just coily enough to wear an awesome Afro. Her hair's fine density and low porosity mean her hair has a hard time holding a curl for a twist out.
>
> **Melissa** would be a 4c on the conventional scale. But on our Hair Checkup cycle, she is kinky hot. Hair like hers, with its thick density and low porosity, is ideal for braid outs and locs. It can also seem stronger than it actually is when, in truth, it is fragile and needs a lot of moisture.
>
> **Sylvia** describes her hair as a mix between kinky medium and kinky mild that would land her roughly in the 4b range on the conventional scale. Her hair loves to go "poof" and turn into a puffy cloud. Her hair's fine density and high porosity make it sensitive to moisture and humidity.

We don't have "good" hair. There's no such thing. We don't have "nappy" hair either. We have *happy* hair that possesses a range of textures, density, and porosity. This is our hair story. But it's also yours as well.

1S *Basic Natural Hair 101*

Follow this basic natural hair 101 checklist to get started with building a healthy hair care routine and then read on for more info:

- Always wrap your hair at night with a satin bonnet, scarf, or do-rag.
- Condition after washing to maintain moisture.
- Pick products that work for you, even if they don't work for everyone else.
- Detangle hair using your fingers or a wide-tooth comb, combing from the ends.
- Do not excessively lather your hair when washing, avoiding roughing up the hair.
- Avoid tight, uncomfortable, or itchy hairstyles.
- Create a natural hair regimen—your hair will thank you!
- Try conditioning your hair before washing (a process called pre-poo)—it works!

The Key Is Consistency

One of the most important things in caring for your natural hair is consistency. Consistency can be demonstrated in two main areas: consistency in hair care practice and consistency in the use of specific hair care products. Let's discuss hair care practices first.

Hair Care Practices

Hair care practices are the habitual techniques you use to maintain your hair, also known as a regimen or routine. You may perform certain hair care practices on a daily, weekly, biweekly, or monthly basis. Examples of hair care practices include pre-poos, shampooing, conditioning/deep conditioning, styling, and trimming split ends.

Depending on your hair and your schedule, you may divide these tasks over a two-day weekend. You may not do all of them. But whatever practices you choose for your regimen, you should follow the same steps over and over again. These are your core steps. Finding the right products for each step is crucial and greatly affects how well your hair detangles and retains moisture, preventing damage. Drastic changes in your core steps or the products you use in the core steps can produce unwanted results, causing unnecessary damage. This is why it is important to be selective when changing or choosing new hair products.

The start of a new year is an ideal time to examine your hair routine. Is it working? Why or why not? After asking these questions, you can consider trying new hair products. Branching out from your staples can seem scary at first, but you may find there are other products that your hair will enjoy even more.

Overall, keep it simple! Shorten your hair routine so that it only contains a few steps. Were you short on time to do your hair last year? Combining and simplifying steps can be a way to speed up your natural hair regimen. In other words, make your hair regimen flexible to fit your natural hair's needs and your schedule.

Dos & Don'ts of Hair Care Regimens

1. Never Skip Deep Conditioning

You can get away with skipping a rinse-out conditioner, but not a deep conditioner because it contributes to your overall moisture retention.

Time-saving tip: buy deep conditioners or masques instead of making your own.

2. Avoid Dangerous Chemicals

Get into the habit of reading the ingredient lists on your products. If they contain harmful ingredients like mineral oil, polymers, PEGs, or fragrance, consider replacing them.

Time-saving tip: read company policies online to see which businesses pledge to include organic and natural ingredients in their products.

3. Break It Up Over Friday and Saturday

Divide your hair care regimen into steps over the weekend. Friday can be your take-down day and Saturday your wash day.

Time-saving tip: Dedicate two to four hours of your morning or evening to caring for your hair.

4. Learn New Hairstyles

Headbands used to be my main go-to for my updo hairstyles. I placed them on my hair and *voila*!—instant hairstyle. The result was breakage along my hairline. Stop using accessories that damage your hair to style hair and research other hairstyle alternatives. Be creative in the types of styles you choose and choose which ones work best for your hair health.

Time-saving tip: practice a hairstyle until you can reduce the time it takes to style it or find a trusted friend or natural hair beautician to style your hair for you.

2S   *It's all about the scalp.*

While types of hair differ from person to person, all of our scalps are the same and there are some general dos and don'ts that everyone should follow. It takes a labor of self-love to consistently give your scalp what it needs to be healthy and to grow healthy hair.

The scalp is at the root of it all. Really. Without a healthy scalp, it's difficult for hair to thrive. Got dandruff? Does your scalp itch or flake? Does it have sores or pus-filled bumps? All tell-tale signs that something is amiss. When the scalp is not healthy, hair beware.

Now, there are lots of things that can impact your scalp and cause issues. Some of them include poor styling practices. Have you ever burned your scalp while straightening your hair? Heat damage. Have you taken too long to wash your hair and weeks have slipped by? Product buildup.

Internal and external health of the scalp are both important because, like tilling the soil for a harvest, a healthy scalp yields healthy hair.

Internal Health

Omega-3 oil found in fish (salmon), eggs, and nuts can be very helpful in maintaining a premium scalp. The fatty acids in the oil keep the scalp moisturized and can ward off dry scalp as well as combat dandruff. Omega-3 oil can also be consumed in vitamins with added benefits like boosting immunity and brain function.

When it comes to the scalp, reducing inflammation is key because it allows the scalp to rest during the hair follicle growth cycle without causing irritation or redness. That's why food and spices like ginger, calendula, and turmeric are powerful superfoods for the scalp. Ginger aids in blood circulation; calendula and turmeric both reduce inflammation stress. According to the renowned herbalist Rosemary Gladstar's *Herbal Recipes for Vibrant Health*, calendula heals "the body by promoting cell repair."[1]

External Health

When it comes to external care, a lot can be done to maintain optimum scalp health. For example, tight braiding, tight weaves, and cornrowing can cause scarring and bumps on the scalp. Washing styling tools goes a long way. Not washing hair scarves or satin pillowcases can cause scalp irritations as old oil, grease, and germs weigh on the skin. That's why it's important to ditch old scarves or to wash that satin bonnet with each wash cycle before placing it over newly washed hair.

Washing your hair in general is important too: regular washing combats products from building up on the surface of the scalp after regular rotations of styling. Choose a natural shampoo made with castor oil, aloe vera juice, or black soap to gently cleanse the scalp without drying it out. Greasing the scalp is not necessary—it's an old practice.

If you're still using an old-school pantyhose stocking cap to cover your hair before you go to sleep, it's also time to update your sleepwear. The best option to protect your hair at night is a satin pillowcase, satin bonnet, or scarf. Satin is a lot more delicate on your scalp and doesn't absorb all the oil so your scalp stays hydrated and your hair retains moisture while you sleep, preventing snagging and breakage. Are you a heavy sleeper? Opt for a do-rag or a satin bonnet with ties that you can lace around your head to secure it in place.

For those dry scalp days (because we all have them), try adding grapeseed oil mixed with tea tree essential oil for dandruff or jojoba oil for general dryness concerns. The great thing about jojoba oil is that it doesn't become rancid easily and the oil is similar to sebum, the natural hair oil our scalps naturally make. Simply apply straight to dry areas. It's a win-win.

When it comes to healthy hair, start with maintaining a healthy scalp.

3S Four Ways You May Be Damaging Your Scalp

Avoid these common hair care mistakes to ensure that your scalp is healthy and thriving:

1. **Scratching your scalp with your fingernails.** Your nails carry dirt and bacteria underneath them. When you scratch your scalp, you transfer those germs onto a fragile part of your hair. Scratching can also damage the scalp by creating abrasions or cuts that can turn into scabs.

2. **Ignoring scalp irritation.** When your scalp itches or becomes irritated, it is often a sign of improper cleansing. Ignoring scalp irritation can lead to issues like dandruff, a dry scalp, or an excessively oily scalp. Focus on cleansing your scalp when you wash your hair. After washing your hair, moisturize your scalp with natural oils like jojoba oil, sweet almond oil, or grapeseed oil. Add four to six drops of tea tree essential oil to your oil mixture; it protects against bacteria and fungus.

3. **Improper Cleansing.** So, you wash your hair, but are you doing it correctly? Cleaning the scalp is the most important part of the hair-washing routine. A scalp clogged with product buildup and oil does not foster healthy hair growth. Make sure to wash your hair with a non-sulfate shampoo. Massage your scalp with your fingertips while washing. Examine your scalp after washing to ensure that there is no buildup left.

4. **Irregular Washing.** Washing your hair infrequently can also lead to a dirty, unhealthy scalp. Set a routine day to wash your hair. Some don't need to wash their hair as often as others. Find a hair wash routine that works best for you.

4S   Damaging Styling Practices

Avoid these common damaging styling practices to ensure that your hair stays healthy:

Using the Wrong Comb

If you don't have a wide-tooth comb, I highly suggest that you get one. Or you can finger detangle instead (see Salon Chair Session 11S "Use Your Fingers"). Either way, using the wrong type of comb can greatly damage your hair by pulling it and causing major breakage to the hair strands. Narrow-tooth combs like rattail combs are great for parting and dividing the hair into sections, but the rule of thumb for natural hair should be the wider the spaces between the "teeth" of the comb, the better. That's because wide-tooth combs allow you to detangle knots gently with less likelihood of snagging the hair.

Using a Hot Comb That Can Burn the Scalp

I know we can all remember some form of the hot comb whether it was used on our hair or a family member's. However, the hot comb is not best practice when it comes to caring for natural hair. Besides the fact that the comb's teeth are narrow, which we have already discussed is a no-no, the heat from hot-combing your hair can cause thinning over time and not to mention scalp burns and heat damage in general.

Flat-Ironing Hair to a Crisp

Flat-ironing once or twice a year is okay when the heat setting isn't too high. Most stylists recommend choosing a heat setting that is between 340 to 370 degrees for fine or color-treated hair and 350 to 400 degrees for medium to coarse hair. However, over time, flat-ironing can lead to hair loss or damaged hair strands.

Keeping in Weaves, Wigs, or Extensions Too Long

The same goes for weaves, wigs, and other extensions. Brevity like four weeks is fine, but leaving in braids or weaves for months on end can cause breakage and thin your own natural hair underneath. I would also limit the use of weaves altogether if after taking your hair down it is thinning or has suffered breakage. Wigs can be taken off daily, but it should be noted that wearing a wig cap continuously underneath the wig can cause damage if worn too tightly or if proper hygiene is not maintained.

Not Combing from the Ends

Natural hair is not like the straight-haired doll hair you might have combed as a child. It has to be combed from the ends. To do this, part your hair into four to six sections and apply a leave-in conditioner or detangler product. Using your wide-tooth comb, hold each section individually and begin combing, starting at the end of the hair first and then making your way up toward the scalp. I recommend always detangling natural hair when you are deep conditioning or when your hair has a leave-in conditioner in it because this allows the comb to slip through the strands, avoiding unnecessary breakage.

Not Using Protective Hairstyles

If you find yourself tempted to style or not style your hair in a particular way because you are unsure of what others may think, it is time to take a step back and rethink your motives. The Bible tells us to seek the favor of God and not the favor of men. When you choose to change or not change your hair based on the thoughts of others, your focus is not on your Creator. Never sacrifice your hair's health or stop yourself from trying something new to fit into a look or style you think will please others. In other words, if your hair needs a protective hairstyle, do it without reservations.

Work to be the best you can be because you value your personal uniqueness in Christ and not because you need people's approval to feel worthwhile.

5S   *Hair Cleansers, Cleansing Washes*

Move over, shampoo! Your everyday shampoo is not the only way to remove dirt and product buildup and to effectively cleanse your scalp. Try these lesser-known hair cleansers, washes, and rinses to maintain clean hair and a clean scalp:

Water

Water is the best moisturizer you can use! If you live in an area with hard water (water filled with minerals that can harm your hair), you can use distilled water instead.

Apple Cider Vinegar

Along with a cleansing shampoo, another option to use with a shampoo is apple cider vinegar diluted in water.

Black Soap

Liquid black soap is a mild scalp/hair cleanser (the soap bar is not the best because it can carry bacteria between washes). It can be a gentle cleansing, low-chemical shampoo that clarifies the scalp.

Herbal Tea Infusion

Boil the water in a tea kettle. Meanwhile, place two tea bags in a heat-safe Pyrex glass measuring cup. Pour the hot water over the two tea bags and let them steep, covered for three to five minutes or until the water darkens. Remove the tea bags carefully. For loose-leaf tea or fresh herbs, I would recommend soaking your tea in a coffee strainer set in a heat-safe container to get the maximum amount of saturation. If using the tea for hair, do not add honey.

Pour the herb-infused water over your hair, collecting the water in another bowl. Pour the collected water over your hair again. Rinse your hair thoroughly with cold water and style as usual. Make sure to thoroughly rinse your hair with cool water after using the rinse. I think for kinky/coily hair, tea rinses are more effective when rinsed out like a regular conditioner.

Aloe Vera Juice

Aloe vera juice can be diluted with water and, similar to an herbal tea rinse, poured over your hair after shampooing to add an extra boost of hydration.

Coconut Milk/Coconut Oil

Coconut milk or coconut oil can be used as a pre-poo (see Glossary) to strengthen and nourish dry, damaged natural hair.

Rosewater/Flower Waters

You can also mix rosewater or other "flower waters" (also known as hydrosols) with distilled water and use them to rinse your hair after washing. Feel free to add your favorite conditioner as well for an extra hydration boost. I recommend incorporating flower waters a little bit at a time into your regimen by testing them on a small section of hair before using it all over.

6S Wash Day

Wash day. The most infamous day. It can take all day, involve multiple steps, and before you know it, your weekend revolves around setting up your hair appointment or having a cleaning and styling session. For us, washing our hair isn't usually a part of the shower experience. Doing hair is planned, organized, and schedule-clearing. Wash day can be daunting if you have hair that easily tangles and tightly curls up.

Reframe your perspective on washing your hair and think of it as relaxing and a fulfilling act of service for your hair. The circular scalp massaging, scent of the shampoo, and warmth of the water are relaxing. Consistency in washing your hair is so significant. Straight hair can be washed more often, even daily. But for coily hair, less washing is actually best. Limiting wash days to once a week, once every two weeks, or once a month is much better treatment for kinky hair. How often you wash your hair and how you do it depends on your hair needs. Some people swear by washing their hair once a week, while for others, once a month is better. The best way to figure out what works for you is to test it out. After a while, you will be able to tell how long you can go before needing to wash your hair.

Not washing hair daily can seem strange to people without naturally kinky or coily hair. Some may think our natural hair is dirty or messy because it does not have to be washed as often as straight hair, but this is not only biased but also ignorant thinking. Young girls may go to school and be teased for their natural hair and can face criticism by misplaced comments. It is important to teach girls about the glorious differences of natural hair so that they do not easily succumb to the opinions and subjectivity of others. Ultimately, what others think truly doesn't matter.

Ways to tell it is time to wash your hair can be if your hair has an odor or has dandruff or flakes on the scalp. It is a good idea to start a regular hair-washing rotation or cycle and to keep track of when it is time to wash your hair on a calendar.

Steps for washing natural hair include shampoo, conditioner, and deep conditioner. I recommend using a sulfate-free, natural shampoo formulated with aloe vera juice or natural oils that won't dry out hair. While most people are familiar with the shampoo and conditioning process of washing hair, for natural hair, it is best to add a step called pre-poo (see Glossary).

As a mother (Shelia here), I always saved the shampooing for the last step when I bathed my children when they were babies because as soon as it was done, my little ones would fall into a nice long nap when I rubbed their little scalps in a circular motion.

Wash and Moisturize Regularly

Taking the time to regularly wash and moisturize your natural hair should be a priority. Moisturizing your hair is also important if you want to protect it. The problem is we become tired, life stresses us out, or we really are overwhelmed with an ever-surmounting stack of tasks on our to-do list. That's when it is time to cool the breaks, take a step back, and enlist some help. I recommend reaching out to a stylist or close family member or friend who is experienced with natural hair and can style and tend your hair for you.

Or you can wash, moisturize, and then use a wig, weave, or extensions as temporary options until you have time to style. However, do not make these a regular fallback; monitor how long you keep them in your hair so you don't damage it.

Use a calendar to track how often you wash and moisturize your natural hair. It can lead to long-term benefits. By washing your hair regularly, you can prevent product buildup on your scalp, stop sores or bumps from being produced, and emotionally feel better that your hair is clean.

How to Pre-poo Natural Hair

A pre-poo or pre-shampoo is a treatment applied to the hair before shampooing/washing. Pre-poo treatments can be done with oil or with a conditioner.

Benefits of Pre-poo treatments

- helps in detangling hair
- nourishes scalp and roots
- protects fragile ends of hair
- keeps moisture locked into hair while washing
- prevents shampoo from "stripping" natural oils from hair

Pre-pooing with Oil

First, select a carrier oil that works best with your hair (see Salon Chair Session 41S "Carrier & Essential Oils"). Examples of carrier oils that work well for pre-poo treatments include extra virgin olive oil, coconut oil, and, my personal favorite, grapeseed oil. Divide your hair into four to six twists. Untwist each section one at a time and apply oil from root to tip before retwisting. Place a plastic shower cap over the hair for thirty minutes. Shampoo/wash hair as usual.

You can use a small amount of oil to do a pre-poo, style your hair, and lightly moisturize it. How much oil you will use depends on your hair and how it reacts with the oil. If you have fine hair, it's best to use oil during your pre-poo because you can rinse off the excess oil when you wash your hair. People with thick, coarse hair may prefer using oil to moisturize/style their hair after it has been washed.

Pre-pooing with Conditioner

Select a water-based conditioner that is easy to spread throughout your hair. To check if your conditioner has water in it, read the ingredients on the product. The first ingredient should say "distilled water." Follow the same steps as if you were prepooing with oil. Shampoo/wash hair as usual.

Which is better for a pre-poo: oil or conditioner?

Oil is the best option for a pre-poo because it is inexpensive and readily available in local grocery stores. I am able to purchase a large bottle of oil and use it for months. Conditioners can be expensive—especially if they include organic, vegan, or natural ingredients. Inexpensive conditioners can contain synthetic ingredients that coat the hair and conceal damage to the hair structure. In contrast, oils naturally condition and nourish the hair.

7S   Sample Healthy Hair Care Regimen & Calendar

When I first started my natural hair journey, I frequently wrote down what worked for my hair. After a while, I stopped.

Result: I easily forgot my past mistakes or hair care routines that worked for me. Sometimes I ended up making the same hair care mistake.

Solution: Document! It's easy to forget how far you've come, but if you keep track, you will be amazed and encouraged by your results. Below is a sample regimen/routine.

Every one to two days: moisturize and seal your hair with a leave-in conditioner or oil.

Nighttime: sleep wearing a satin bonnet, scarf, or cap, and/or use a silk or satin pillowcase.

Weekly/biweekly: Pre-poo, shampoo, and condition/deep condition your hair (in that order) to cleanse, rehydrate, and restore moisture to your hair. A clay treatment (aka, "mud" wash) is an optional step to maintain and strengthen your hair's elasticity. While the deep conditioner is in your hair, detangle it with a wide-tooth comb for optimal slip. Finally, use a water-based leave-in conditioner, oil, and styling cream/butter (think Liquid-Conditioner-Oil or LOC) that suits your hair density to "loc" in moisture.

Monthly or quarterly: Do a special protein treatment with clays, powders, or henna to maintain hair health. Also, trim split ends.

Sunday	Monday	Tuesday	Wednesday	Thursday	Friday	Saturday
	1	2	3	4	5	6
Style for the week	Moisturize	Moisturize	Moisturize	Moisturize	Moisturize	Pre-poo/ Shampoo, (Deep) Condition, LOC
7	8	9	10	11	12	13
Style for the week	Moisturize	Moisturize	Moisturize	Moisturize	Moisturize	
14	15	16	17	18	19	20
Style for the week	Moisturize	Moisturize	Moisturize	Moisturize	Moisturize	Pre-poo/ Shampoo, (Deep) Condition, LOC
21	22	23	24	25	26	27
Style for the week	Moisturize	Moisturize	Moisturize	Moisturize	Moisturize	Special Protein Treatment
28	29	30				
(Protective) Style for the week	Moisturize	Moisturize				

Figure 1. Sample Hair Care Regimen Calendar.

8S *Dandruff*

A lot of people, including me (Sylvia), struggle with dandruff and flaky scalps. Dandruff and flaky scalps can be caused by oiliness, product buildup, stress, hormonal imbalance, and even factors like weather and diet.

If you're experiencing dandruff, evaluate the hair products you are using. Evaluate the content and results of these products as well.

Are you using a sulfate-free shampoo? Sulfate-free shampoos do not contain harsh chemicals that can further damage and dry out the scalp.

Does your conditioner/leave-in contain synthetic ingredients? Use a conditioner that does not contain mineral oil or petroleum, both of which are synthetic ingredients that can clog pores in the scalp, leading to dandruff.

Are the special treatments you're using helpful or harmful? Apple cider vinegar, tea tree essential oil, and other acidic products are all popular options for naturally treating a scalp suffering from dandruff and itchiness. However, you must evaluate the results of these products as well.

Apple Cider Vinegar Rinses:

Apple cider vinegar (ACV) rinses can be too harsh for some hair types. Always dilute the vinegar beforehand and evaluate your scalp after rinsing. *Is the scalp red or irritated after the ACV rinse?* If so, discontinue use.

Tea Tree Oil:

Are you using authentic, organic tea tree essential oil? The ingredients list on the back of the product should *only* say: *melaleuca alternifolia oil.* Melaleuca alternifolia is the scientific name for tea tree. Anything else is not real tea tree oil. Real tea tree essential oil is also packaged in glass. (Essential oils have to be packaged in glass so that they do not react with plastic.)

9S Swim Day

To be blunt, I (Shelia) *hated* swim day. I went to high school in the seventies when we had to wear the standard blue one-piece gym jumpsuit and had a weekly inspection by our gym teacher to see if our jumpsuit had been ironed. We couldn't have a wrinkled suit. More than I hated pressing that blue gym jumpsuit before inspection on Friday, I hated swim day on Mondays. A few Mondays, I hid in the gym locker room to avoid swim day. My favorite excuse for not swimming was "it's that time of the month." It wasn't the activity of swimming I dreaded but that my hair would get wet and the chlorine would make it dry, dull, and lifeless. I especially hated that white swim cap that buckled under the chin. It never held my hair snug enough especially around the nape of my neck when I would float backward. I was put off from swimming because it caused the ongoing battle of dealing with my hair.

Swim Caps for Natural Hair

Now, years later, to read about swim caps designed just for natural Afro hair is liberating. A swimming cap made specifically for natural Afro hair has received official approval from the International Swimming Federation (FINA), which administers international water sports competitions, including during the Olympics.[1] This is a big step forward for kinky hair because, in general, wearing a swim cap while swimming can aid in preventing chlorine damage.

Caring for Natural Hair Post Chlorinated or Saline Water

Before swimming, consider doing a cowash (see Glossary), which will help your hair absorb less chlorinated water and keep it conditioned while you enjoy your swim. For swim hairstyles, braid or twist your natural hair before swimming to prevent it from becoming tangled.

After swimming, wash and cleanse your hair as you would do normally. Keep in mind, though, you should rinse your hair thoroughly with cold water, as this will help the hair cuticles lay flat and retain moisture.

If you swim frequently, do a cowash instead of shampooing. This will prevent your hair from becoming dry from extra washes. Also, once a month, consider using a clarifying shampoo to aid in the removal of any buildup of chlorine chemicals. Always follow up a clarifying shampoo with a conditioner and deep conditioner for kinky or dry hair to ensure the hair does not lose moisture. Consider using a shampoo and conditioner with organic/natural ingredients.

After washing, conditioning, and applying a moisturizing leave-in conditioner, don't forget to also seal your hair with your favorite oil—jojoba oil, grapeseed oil, coconut oil, olive oil, or avocado oil, to name a few—but feel free to choose the best oil for your hair.

10S *Treat Your Hair with Kindness*

Imagine that you are tending a garden. Instead of using water, you pour soda on your little seedling. You hide your plant in the shade where it can't get any sunlight. Weeks go by and your plant begins to wither and fade. "What went wrong?" "Why isn't it growing?" Sounds silly, right? Everyone knows plants need water and lots of sunlight, not soda and shade. But we have all been guilty of sometimes treating our hair the same way. How many times have you forgotten to wash or moisturize your hair or ignored its brittle state because you had other things to do?

The first step in caring for natural hair is realizing that it is a growing organism. Hair has a growth and death cycle. Just as a plant, a young seedling, needs to be cared for with generous watering and rays of golden sunlight, your hair needs moisture and vitamins to properly nourish it.

Moisture

One of the biggest myths in hair care is that water is drying. Not true! In fact, water is at the top of the list of good moisturizers for hair. There are several other liquids you can incorporate into your hair care routine to remoisten it.

Aloe vera juice
Coconut milk
Rosewater/flower waters

Strengthen/Feeding with Protein Products for Natural Hair

Treat your hair with protein-enriching clays, powders, and foods on a monthly basis to strengthen your hair strands.

  Alma powder
  Bentonite clay
  Blackstrap molasses
  Cassia obovata
  Greek yogurt
  Honey
  Rhassoul clay

Vitamins that provide essential nutrients to make your hair healthy from the inside out and for hair growth

  Biotin
  Magnesium
  Omega–3
  Turmeric
  Vitamin C

Trim/Prune

Regularly cut your hair's split ends. Use the twist-and-snip method or get them professionally cut. And remember to be gentle with your hair. Use styling tools like a wide-tooth comb, or better—your fingers, to unravel tangles.

Seal Natural Ends

Coat your hair ends with sealing butters or pomades to seal in moisture and prevent dryness and breakage.

Cupuacu
Cocoa
Kokum
Mango
Murumuru
Shea

Shelter and Protect Your Natural Hair

Guard your hair from cold or hot weather by wearing protective hairstyles in the winter and sun hats or turbans in the summer.

11S   *Use Your Fingers*

When it comes to taking care of natural hair, your hands can be your biggest help or your ultimate downfall. Many naturals are too rough when handling their hair and when applying products. Hence the term "heavy-handed," which was a term for beauticians who caused pain when detangling kinky hair or straightening it with the hot comb, is recoined today by naturals who excessively use products.

Natural hair is fragile and needs to be nurtured and handled with care. The best tools to detangle, style, and groom natural hair are fingers.

Long-tooth combs and soft-hair brushes are helpful, but using your fingers allows you to be gentler with your hair. Also, when applying products, using your fingers allows you to follow the "finger test" (see below) to measure the right amount of products to put on your hair each time.

For moisturizers, creams, and butters, use a dollop the size of your pointer finger (or close to the size of a dime) for each section of hair you moisturize.

For gels, pomades, and sealants, use a dollop the size of your pinky finger for each section of hair, focusing primarily on the ends of the tresses.

Once I (Sylvia) started finger detangling, using a comb was not always necessary. I still have my collection of various detangling combs and picks, but I love using my hands.

12S   Protective Hairstyles

A protective hairstyle is a style that "protects" or safeguards the hair from damage. Protective hairstyles include braids, crochet extensions, clip-ins, weaves, and wigs. Since head scarves cover the hair, they can also be used as a protective style.

To clarify, "out" styles are the opposite of protective hairstyles. They include the likes of fros, twist outs, braid outs, or anything where your hair is out.

"Semi-protective" means a hairstyle that includes a combination of hair that is out and hair that is tucked away, whether in braids, twists, or extensions.

Protective hairstyles can be worn year-round. They are great for "protecting" the fragile ends of your natural hair from the environment. Protective hairstyles also help your hair maintain moisture for longer periods of time. And finally, protective hairstyles look professional and can be worn in the workplace.

Below are three professional protective natural hairstyles for work.

Flat Twist Bantu Knot Out Updo

Updos are perfect for work because they keep your hair out of your face, which allows you to focus on the tasks at hand instead of worrying about whether or not your hair is askew. Flat twists and Bantu knots are ideal for creating curls that can be pinned or tucked away with the help of a few bobby pins.

Recommended hair length: short or medium
Suggested materials: rat tail comb, foaming mousse, hair butter
Instructions: Part and flat twist the back of your hair going up. Bantu knot the ends. Bantu knot the front of your natural hair.

Flat Twist and Twist Out Combo

Twist outs have become a classic and instant staple for most women with natural hair. That's because they are easy, require little styling experience, and can be restyled in the middle of the week if necessary. For a flat twist out, some practice will be required. For beginners, however, a simple twist out can be styled on medium-length hair and worn for three days before having to do a touch-up. Be sure to gently retwist your hair at night and wear a satin bonnet while sleeping in order to maintain the style.

Recommended hair length: medium
Suggested materials: rat tail comb, foaming mousse, hair butter
Instructions: Part and flat twist the front of your hair. Twist the ends. Twist the back of your natural hair.

Side Flat Twist

Side flat twists are exactly how they sound: you flat twist your hair on one side and let the rest of the hair hang, creating a waterfall effect. This hairstyle is great for those with long or curly natural hair. I recommend rolling the twisted ends of your hair with flexi rods overnight before taking it down in the morning before work to reveal springy curls.

Recommended hair length: long
Suggested materials: rat tail comb, foaming mousse, hair butter
Instructions: Part and flat twist the side of your natural hair going to the left. Twist the ends toward the front. Flat twist the back going up. Bantu knot the ends.

13S *Being about Head Wraps*

There has been a lot of history about the origins of African-American women wearing headscarves. Let's delve into those facts here. According to *Hair Story: Untangling the Roots of Black Hair in America*, "when an outbreak of ringworm occurred, slaves commonly tied a rag around their heads to cover the unsightly scabs left by the affliction." Later on, rags would also be used by women to cover braids. Eventually, after Emancipation, straight hair became synonymous with "modernity" and "implied education," while "braided hairstyles covered with a head rag branded one countrified and backward."[1] Wearing head scarves has its roots also in colonial America, specifically Louisiana, where black women were legally required to cover their hair. As an act of resistance, black women wore their headscarves in beautiful, fashionable styles to still express their beauty.[2] Different African cultures also have traditional ways to wrap their hair.

The reality now is that headscarves and wraps can be stylish and chic. I (Melissa here) receive compliments on my head scarves when I wear them. It's an accessory that shows your personality. Head scarves can be a great accessory during months of cold weather or even just for running errands. You heard me! Ditch that baseball cap and wrap a turban or scarf around your hair instead. Not a fan of wrapping? Silk-lined turbans that can be slipped over the hair have hit the market and you can now achieve a polished look without the fuss of wrapping or tying a scarf. Plus, with the silk lining, your natural hair is not snagged by the fabric and instead can be protected in a safe cocoon.

Head wraps can also be ideal for protective hairstyles or those recovering from alopecia. The bonus benefit is that head scarves can also be easily removed at the end of the day to let your natural hair breathe. This differs greatly from other protective hairstyles, which often have a "take-down" process, which if ignored and left in the style too long, can cause damage to the hair and scalp.

When purchasing a head scarf, look for such fabrics as cotton, satin, or silk. Avoid harsh fabrics like wool that could snag the hair. Also avoid fabrics that are not breathable, like polyester.

Select colors and designs that match your personality and lifestyle. Are you a classic-style dresser? Feminine, boho, or edgy? Pick scarves that will readily coordinate with your outfits and that appeal to your own personal sense of style.

Some jobs lend themselves to being a place where head wraps are accepted while others may not view them as readily acceptable. However, overall, I think a head wrap is an elegant and eye-catching option.

14S *Six Reasons You Keep Having Split Ends*

1. **You comb your hair too much.** Combing your hair too frequently can cause damage, aka split ends. Try finger detangling instead.

2. **You don't deep condition enough.** Proper deep conditioning is crucial for maintaining moisturized, healthy hair. Hair that has a balance of moisture and protein is less susceptible to breakage.

3. **You use too many bobby pins.** While a great asset to hairstyles, bobby pins that are used to pin up ends of the hair can cause snagging and breakage. Try doing styles that don't require bobby pins.

4. **You don't trim your hair regularly.** When you find a split end or fairy knot, cut it off. Avoiding trims won't help you in the long run. In fact, not trimming will prevent length retention.

5. **You use too many protein products.** Although products or treatments with proteins (e.g., keratin, henna) add strength to your hair, without a proper balance of moisture, your hair can become brittle.

6. **You aren't lubricating your ends.** Always treat your ends with care, putting the heaviest amount of product on them to keep them happy, conditioned, and strong.

15 S   *Superior Ways to Moisturize Natural Hair Year-Round*

When hot weather starts up, it can cause our natural hair to become dry, brittle, or puffy and frizzy with humidity. Alternatively, the winter months can be the most *freezing* cold time of the year! Even though the cold weather brings with it a time for seasonal activities and get-togethers, it can be rough on your hair. Below are ways to combat the heat and save your hair from the sun and the cold.

Hydrate

Drink at least four cups of water each day; six cups is better.[1] The more water our bodies consume, the more moisture our natural hair is able to maintain throughout the day. Avoid water with additives like salt or flavoring and instead drink purified drinking water. Read your ingredient list to see what is listed.

Omega-3 Fish Oil

Take an Omega-3 fish oil tablet daily. Omega-3 fish oil, found naturally in fish like salmon and sardines as well as in flaxseeds, can replenish your natural hair with needed nutrients. The fish oil will help your hair as well as your skin stay moisturized when outside in the sun. Invest in high-quality Omega-3 tablets that have been certified as being free of environmental toxins or metals. Start with a small amount and make sure you drink a lot of water when taking any vitamins to adequately move the nutrients throughout your system. And of course, always consult your doctor before taking any vitamin or supplement.

Flaxseed Gel

Make your own homemade flaxseed gel following a recipe. Flaxseed gel coats your natural hair shaft on the outside, creating a protective coating that will help your hair resist the heat of the sun's rays. Flaxseed gel will also keep your hair spongy and soft as well as define your natural curl pattern. Use flaxseed gel with a butter or natural styling foam mousse for flat twists, Bantu knots, and twist out hairstyles.

Sesame Seed Oil

Use sesame seed oil to pre-shampoo, deep condition, and apply to the scalp and ends of the hair after washing. It is high in many nutrients and vitamins that aid in healthy kinky hair including magnesium, iron, phosphorus, vitamin B1, and zinc. Sesame seed oil strengthens the hair cuticle and naturally increases elasticity. Sesame seed oil is also resistant to going rancid easily. Moreover, it nourishes dry, brittle hair, protects hair from harmful UV rays, heals scalp infections due to its antibacterial properties, prevents dandruff, dry scalp, and strengthens hair from the inside out.

Sesame seed oil is great for fine and coarse, naturally kinky hair as it does not weigh fine hair down and provides sheen and luster to dry hair.

Special note: Always store oils in cool, dark places like kitchen cabinets. Do not store in the bathroom as this can decrease the shelf life of the oil.

16S Two Steps to Regrow Natural Hair

Two simple strategies can help regrow your natural hair. These steps are particularly for those who are experiencing CCCA and are both strategies that Melissa incorporates into her regular hair routine.

Step 1: Clean Scalp and Hair

Clean both your scalp and your hair. The order of this is important. The scalp must be cleaned regularly (once a week or twice a month for African-American natural hair) to prevent buildup of bacteria. Don't worry if other people are alarmed about this. Kinky hair does not have to be washed daily or multiple times a week. This may seem strange to others who may be critical of black hair, but it is actually what is best for our hair.

For those wearing protective hairstyles like wigs and extensions, it is an absolute necessity that the scalp be cleaned with a gentle, cleansing, low-chemical shampoo that clarifies the scalp. Look for shampoos without a lot of chemicals and that contain hydrosols, like aloe vera hydrosol. Plain aloe vera juice works as well. Shampoos should also be rich in oils and butters that promote kinky hair health like mango butter, coconut oil, almond oil, grapeseed oil, and essential oils of peppermint and rosemary. Remember: don't just trust the advertisement hype on the front of the container. Always read the ingredient list to see exactly what you are getting.

To clean the scalp and to shampoo your hair, wet your hair and then focus on adding the shampoo directly to the scalp. Leave it on for a few moments and then gently massage the scalp and roots with your fingertips and palms. Squeeze any excess shampoo from your hair starting at the roots and going toward the ends, being careful not to scrub so that you avoid tangling your hair. Follow up by rinsing the hair thoroughly.

If your scalp is already suffering from open sores, bleeding bumps, itchy red patches, or hot burning sensations, do not apply a harsh cleanser to the scalp. Instead, use a gentle calendula and ginger mask or Manuka honey (medicinal grade) with a High-Active of 12–15+ or liquid black soap as a mild scalp/hair cleanser.

Recipe: Ginger and Calendula Hair Mask for Inflamed Scalps

Ingredients
- ⅛ teaspoon ginger powder
- ¼ teaspoon calendula flower powder
- 1 tablespoon raw honey

Instructions
1. Mix calendula flower powder, ginger powder, and raw honey together.
2. Apply the paste to the scalp and leave on for 10–20 minutes.
3. Wash hair with a gentle black soap shampoo.

Note: You can substitute chamomile tea leaves for the calendula flower powder.

Along with a cleansing shampoo, other options to use are apple cider vinegar diluted in water or a mixture containing cleansing clays like bentonite. Tea tree essential oil is known for being antibacterial, but should be diluted before use. The rule of thumb for an apple cider vinegar rinse is to use 3 parts water to 1 part vinegar. Apply the rinse after shampooing and then rinse thoroughly.

Recipe: Aloe Vera Gel Leave-in Conditioner

- 4 oz. water
- 4 oz. aloe vera gel
- 10 drops of essential oil (pick your favorite!)

Directions: Add water and aloe vera gel to a small bowl and stir lightly with a spoon. Pour the contents into a spray bottle and shake. Add an essential oil of your choice and shake lightly again. Use daily or as often as needed to restore softness.

Step 2: Assess and Solve

It is important to understand the cause behind the inflammation of the scalp and to assess recent hairstyle choices.

Next, begin to eliminate these hair styling techniques and replace them with healthier ones.

Scalp-inflaming hairstyles	Healthier styles to replace scalp-inflaming hairstyles
Tight braids	Looser braids or flat twists
Heavy/tight extensions	Loose braids, lightweight extensions like crochet hair
Glue-in weaves	Comfortable clip-ins
Wig caps	Loose-fitting wig caps that are washed regularly
Braided tracks under weaves	Looser braids and crochet curls or crochet braids
Hot-combing	Flat-ironing at recommended setting
Chemical relaxing	Flat-ironing at recommended setting
Oiling/greasing the scalp	Using jojoba oil
Tight rollers or curlers	Flexi Rods
Blow-drying	Allow hair to air dry

Consult a dermatologist who can examine your scalp and determine the underlying cause and the proper solutions.

17S   Hair Growth & Perceptions That Come with It

Not everyone can grow the same length of hair, but everyone can aim to grow their version of healthy hair. Your hair might not be growing longer due to chemical damage, breaking off due to a hairstyle or coloring, or poor nutrition. Other factors that impact hair growth include age and genetics. To summarize the science of it all, everyone's hair is different and many factors influence how fast your hair grows.

"What Makes You Beautiful" by the UK boy band One Direction was one of the biggest pop hits of 2011. However, the lyrics of the song have connotations that potentially alienate a large portion of the female audience. The point of the song is simple: being beautiful is equated with being humble and not vain about your looks. Yet, the lyrics mention a girl flipping her hair over her shoulder to target a select group of females. Not many young girls with Afros or Afro puffs can "flip" their hair.

In the music video for "Whip My Hair" by Willow Smith, a pop hit by a girl with natural hair, she "whips" her hair "back and forth." Notice the difference in the lyrics. No flipping involved. Compared to "What Makes You Beautiful," "Whip My Hair" challenges females to be confident in themselves and their hair by ignoring any haters. It's interesting that a song by an African-American female with natural hair replaces the status quo hair "flip" with "whip." Whipping the hair does not require straight, long hair and has less to do with hair than the freedom to be yourself.

When it comes to hair growth, make sure you are not focused on other people's perceptions of what is the ideal length of hair. Not everyone has "waterfall hair." But everyone can have their *own* beautiful hair.

If you continue to take care of your hair, it will grow. Hair goes through several growing cycles. Most of the time, it is about what goes inside your body, not on your hair, that counts. Try taking a multivitamin or vitamin B supplement like biotin (speak to your doctor first)! Eating healthy daily, sleeping well at night for the recommended number of hours, and exercising all contribute to hair growth and health.

Kinky hair *can* grow long, but why does beauty have to be equated with hair length? The emphasis should not be on length but health. Using protective hairstyles and continuing to care for your hair consistently can improve your hair's ability to retain length.

For general hair growth, keep these two main tips in mind.

Reduce stress: Stress is a huge inhibitor of hair growth. Feeling stressed and pressured to have your hair appear a certain way? Don't increase your stress levels. Research shows that chronic stress can actually cause your hair to fall out quicker.

Eat healthy: I can't emphasize proper nutrition enough; eating foods like fish, nuts, dark green vegetables, and legumes, as well as incorporating biotin into your diet really does go a long way in not only improving your body's overall health but aiding in increasing hair growth too.

In the end, it is your own perception of your natural hair that matters most. Shift your focus from having hair that "flips" and instead do what's best for your body to grow a healthy head of hair.

18S   *Understanding Thickness, Density & Porosity*

Thickness has to do with the width of an individual hair strand. There are three types of hair strands: fine, medium, and coarse. You can determine your natural hair's thickness by comparing a piece of shed hair to a piece of sewing thread:

Fine hair: your individual hair strand is thinner than a piece of sewing thread split in half.
Medium hair: your individual hair strand is the same size as a piece of sewing thread.
Coarse hair: your individual hair strand is larger than a piece of sewing thread.

Density is sometimes confused with thickness. This is an understandable mistake that even seasoned naturals make. Density is the number of individual hair strands a person has on their scalp. Here's how density and thickness relate:

Fine hair strands = very dense hair
Medium hair strands = somewhat dense hair
Coarse hair strands = less dense hair

Knowing your hair's thickness and density will help you to determine what kinds of products to use and how easy it will be for you to distribute them throughout your hair. For instance, if you have fine, thin natural hair that is dense, heavy creams and even some butters will be harder for you to distribute throughout your hair. That's because the denseness of your hair will prevent heavy products from penetrating the sections of your hair. While you can divide your hair into smaller sections and comb the product through each section to ensure that it is evenly distributed, heavy products like shea butter or castor oil will more than likely cause fine natural hair to be limp or overly oily/greasy.

You can use natural products at different stages in your hair routine. Some can be applied to your hair before you shampoo (as a pre-poo), after using a leave-in conditioner, or added to a deep conditioner for extra moisturization.

Products for Fine/Medium Hair

Water-based, creamy leave-in conditioners
Light butters: mango butter
Light oils: jojoba oil, grapeseed oil, almond oil, sunflower oil, argan oil, tamanu oil, sea buckthorn oil, macadamia nut oil, babassu oil
Heavy oils: avocado oil or coconut oil for pre-poos only

Products for Coarse Hair

Thick, water-based, creamy leave-in conditioners
Heavy butters: shea butter, cocoa butter, cupuacu butter
Light butters: mango butter
Light oils: Tamanu oil, sea buckthorn oil, macadamia nut oil, Babassu oil
Heavy oils: avocado oil, coconut oil, olive oil, castor oil
Aloe vera juice
Coconut milk

To find out if your leave-in conditioner is water-based, read the ingredients list. Distilled water, aloe vera juice, hydrosol, aqua, or an aqueous infusion should be the first ingredient.

19S Ways to Grow Out Chemical Treatments & Return to Natural Hair

When you decide to transition to natural hair after having a relaxer, you will have to grow your hair out. The roots of your hair that are not relaxed will naturally have an Afro texture. This is commonly called "new growth."

As your hair transitions, you can use weaves or braids. Eventually, you will have to cut your hair to fully remove the relaxed ends of your hair and to avoid breakage or damage.

During the transitioning process, make sure to maintain a hair routine that consists of conditioning your hair more often and detangling carefully.

The alternative is to do a "big chop," which means to cut off any relaxed hair so only the Afro-textured hair remains.

One main thing to avoid is heat styling. Refrain from using a flat iron, hot comb, or blow dryer while your hair is transitioning as this can cause unnecessary damage.

20S *Energy for My Hair*

Natural hair isn't usually "wash and wear." Other than short, tapered cuts, most of us can't shampoo in the shower, towel dry our hair when we dry our skin, apply a bit of product, and keep it moving. That's because natural hair requires a little more tenderness, love, and care. Internal motivation is key when it comes to natural hair care. And when you're energized, you are excited to style your hair, wash day doesn't feel like a chore, and instead of pulling on a hat before going out the door, you actually put together a cute hairstyle.

So, in other words, staying energized to care for natural hair is *hard*. It's easy to neglect our hair because sometimes we don't have the energy, time, or mental or emotional capacity to care for and style our hair. Friday evenings and Saturdays, rather than detangling and moisturizing, applying jars of hair creams and butters, or squirting hair lotions into our tresses, we're ready to snuggle under covers or nestle on the couch. And if we have to run errands, we throw on a hat, tucking our hair underneath it.

Here are some tips for when you don't have energy for your hair.

Simplify Your Routine

Any woman with natural hair will tell you that an established "go-to" routine is golden. Select a regular rotation of products to use that will cultivate healthy, flourishing hair. Learn which products and which steps work best for your hair. Observe your hair's needs.

Not all products need to be included in a hair routine and some can be excluded for time's sake. For example, when I first went natural, I used hair rinses like aloe vera juice and apple cider vinegar. I also used coconut oil to pre-poo. Now, however, I only use the following steps: shampoo, deep condition, leave-in conditioner, oil, cream/butter, without any hair rinses.

The more you practice your routine, the more skilled you become at selecting which products work best for you and which you can leave out of your process.

Inspire Yourself

I have a favorite blogger who I follow online, and whenever I need a "hairstyle pick-me-up," I am grateful I can check out what she has recently posted about for some much-needed inspiration. Keeping a catalog of must-try hairstyles can help you maintain your motivation. I know for myself the potential of a new hairstyle, accessory, or overall look makes me want to try it out. Mood boards are great for this as well. Make a physical or digital one, whatever works for you, and whenever you are feeling bored, go back to your collection of photos or videos and give yourself permission to try something new.

21S *The Inner Hair Struggle*

Three ways to transform your thinking about your hair.

1. Style your own hair with confidence.

Do not let the fear of what others may think stop you from trying something new. What will attract people is your confidence in yourself and your ability to love the unique God-given attribute only you have to offer.

2. Encourage others.

Sincerely compliment other women about their natural hair. You never know who needs a kind word or uplifting gesture. Encouraging others also shifts the focus away from yourself and allows you to see that who you are as a person matters the most to God.

3. Spend less time visiting "your idol" blogs.

The Bible (Isaiah 44:9-20) tells us that worshipping idols is a sin because it pulls attention away from God, who alone deserves our devotion and praise. The same goes for having "hair idols." Don't compare your natural hair to others. It's one thing to be inspired by someone else's hair and another to feel your hair is somehow inferior because it doesn't look the same way. If you know you will likely drool over a blogger's hairstyle, steer away from visiting her site. Look for other ways to research natural hair. Invest time into learning how to care for your own hair instead of spending hours watching YouTube videos or looking at pictures.

If you find yourself cruising through images of women with natural hair, say to yourself, "She has beautiful hair. Thank you, God, for giving me my unique natural hair." And move on.

22S   Combating Hair Care Fatigue

Hair care fatigue happens when you become tired of taking care of your natural hair. Women who have had natural hair for years and women who are new to having natural hair can both be affected by hair care fatigue. When you lack the motivation, fatigue can lead to carelessness in your hair care routine, which can result in hair breakage, split ends, dry hair, tangles/knots, and impeded hair growth.

Ways to Know You Have Hair Care Fatigue

- You haven't styled your hair in weeks—it takes too long!
- You fall asleep without bothering to wrap your hair for bed.
- During the weekends, you ignore your hair so you don't have to style it.
- You only moisturize your hair when it's super dry and feels like sandpaper.
- You skip doing a deep conditioner and go straight into washing your hair.

Solutions to Hair Care Fatigue

1. **Change how you research natural hair.** Instead of visiting websites, check out books from the library about natural hair. Talk to your natural hair friends about their hair experiences. Look for new ways to become excited about your hair.
2. **Practice time management.** Search for hairstyles that can be done in five to eight minutes. Practice styling your hair

over the weekend until you feel comfortable with performing styles quickly. During the week, style your hair the night before or wake up early in the morning to style it.

3. **Wear a wig, weave, or extensions.** Everyone needs a break from styling their hair. Wear a wig, weave, or extensions to give your hair a rest from constant styling, which can lead to split ends, tangles, and breakage. Weaves and extensions should be kept in no longer than four to six weeks and hair should be washed and moisturized during that time.

Remember all the hard work you have put into taking care of your hair. Don't let hair care fatigue be a setback in achieving your hair goals. Try the solutions above and take control of how you care for your hair.

23S   Five Tips to Take Care of Your Hair as You Age

For beautiful, healthy hair as you age, follow these steps:

1. **Eat well and exercise.** Everything with our bodies is interconnected. If you are not eating healthily, taking your daily supplements, and forgoing exercise, it will impact your hair. Many nutrients from our food help prevent common hair care issues like dandruff, scaly or itchy scalp, and dryness.

2. **Drink lots of water.** Notice that I did not say fluids here. Enjoy your morning cup of coffee or your evening sip of chai, but the main liquid you need to drink for your hair care is water for superior hair moisturization.

3. **Be selective with hair dyes.** Today, it is stylish to wear your salt-and-pepper hair. If you do decide to dye your hair, make sure to use the most natural option. Dyes can be harmful to your hair, so stick to rinse-out dyes. Even consider mixing your own homemade dye using henna.

4. **Be mindful of your hairstyle choices.** Some older women choose to don a wig over thinning hair, but try other styles like braids or twists. You can also opt for a chic headwrap or an elegant turban.

5. **Stay encouraged.** It's easy to give up on your hair care at any stage in the journey. Natural hair seems time-consuming and there is a prevailing belief that it is not manageable. However, with some research, practice, and ideas from caring "naturalistas," you can find routines and methods that work. Once you find your groove, don't lose it!

24S *Kitchen Salon*

When she was a teenager, my daughter Sylvia wanted to learn how to care for her own natural hair. She was already very creative with a love for mixing things and experimenting with substances. So, she began steeping different types of plants to extract particular oils to try out on her hair and skin. Soon our kitchen windowsills were lined with all different-sized jars and types of oil. It seemed like clutter, but it worked. She found the perfect oils that not only worked on her hair but also on many other people with Afro-textured hair. This simple idea of using what she had also led to the development of her own business.

You may be adding up in your mind the expense of certain hair products. Some of us have even become "product junkies," constantly purchasing creams and moisturizers and all sorts of conditioners and pomades. The ongoing expense can become daunting. Sometimes the most expensive elixirs or creams are just bottles of chemicals. Products for natural hair without tons of chemicals are available, but finding items in your kitchen is fun and financially liberating.

Kitchen items *can* be used on your hair, but some kitchen items should be avoided. The research and knowledge that goes into store-bought or salon-sold products do matter. Nevertheless, since not everyone can afford the newest or most popular hair product, if you're on a budget, some everyday kitchen items can be used for hair care. When it comes to supplying your hair with what it needs, look no further than your kitchen to give your kinks, curls, and coils back their spring. For example, mayonnaise and Greek yogurt make great non-conventional alternatives for deep conditioners. Mayonnaise is highly moisturizing while Greek yogurt is packed with protein for your hair. Try combining an even mix of each together for a winning combination. Additionally, olive oil and grapeseed oil can each be used to lock in moisture, while coconut oil works great as a pre-poo treatment when applied to the hair for ten minutes prior to washing.

Remember, everyone's hair is different and what works for someone else could or could not work for you.

25S *Satin is a natural girl's best friend.*

Here's a best-kept secret: before you go to sleep, you need to wrap your hair. I always find it funny how in movies, black women are shown going to sleep at night with a full face of makeup and—double-gasp–no scarf to cover their hair. It's actually not ideal nor is it a best practice to not cover your hair before sleeping.

Sleepwear for Natural Hair

Your natural hair needs to be protected while you sleep. For bedtime, invest in a silk scarf or satin bonnet to place over your hair. Cotton, though soft to the touch for the skin, absorbs oil and can make your hair dry. Stocking caps (remember those?) are also not the best because they are inferior to silk and satin, plus they can be too tight. Silk or satin will not snag your hair while sleeping nor will it rub against it in a way that creates breakage. Silk or satin fabrics are especially helpful in protecting your hairline; just make sure the bonnet or scarf isn't too tight and you're good to go.

If you tend to fall asleep without wrapping your hair, wrap your hair earlier in the day before you become tired. Until a few months ago, I (Sylvia) used a cheap scarf to wrap my hair at night. It always found a way to slip off of my head in the middle of the night. My hair suffered lots of breakage on my edges where my hair would rub against my pillowcase while I slept. I now wear a satin scarf or a satin bonnet. Both stay nice-n-snug—*not tight*—on my head during the night.

Another good idea is to invest in a satin pillowcase to sleep on. Satin pillowcases also prevent the hair from being damaged while sleeping. Make sure the fabric is easy to launder in the wash. If you choose to forgo the bonnet and use the satin pillowcase solo, try moisturizing your hair in the morning instead of at night so that large amounts of oil don't transfer to the pillowcase while you are sleeping.

If you're a heavy sleeper, you can opt for a combination of a satin bonnet/silk scarf and a satin pillowcase. That way, if your bonnet falls off during the night, your pillowcase can be a backup to still protect your hair. Do-rags or bonnets with ties work as well. Just make sure to check the fabric content for a satin-like texture.

26S *Alopecia*

Hair loss is a topic rarely discussed in the natural hair and beauty community. Studies like in the *International Journal of Women's Dermatology* have found that 12 percent of women experience hair loss (female pattern baldness) before age twenty-nine, and by forty-nine years old, the number increases to 25 percent. At the age of sixty-nine, the number of those experiencing hair loss doubles to 41 percent.[1]

Oftentimes, hair loss can cause emotions of fear and anxiety; it can feel isolating. But it should be discussed so that others can find the help they need. According to an article reviewed by Crystal Ugochi Aguh, MD, associate professor of dermatology and director of the ethnic skin program at John Hopkins University, "almost half of black women experience some form of hair loss."[2]

One common form of hair loss among African-American women is central centrifugal cicatricial alopecia (CCCA).

Central Centrifugal Cicatricial Alopecia

Central Centrifugal Cicatricial Alopecia (CCCA) is when the crown portion of the scalp begins to lose hair in a circular pattern and moves outward. CCCA is sometimes called "hot comb alopecia" and can lead to scarring. "Broken hair in the crown area [is] usually mild at first," explains Ife Rodney, a board-certified dermatologist in Fulton, Maryland. "This usually begins to happen when patients are in their early 30s, she says, though she's seen women in their 20s come in for CCCA treatment as well."[3]

The risk of experiencing CCCA is increased by the following hairstyles/treatments: hot-combing, chemical relaxing; chronic use of braids, extensions, and weaves, tight rollers or curlers; and excessive blow-drying. All of these are damaging hair styling practices because they can cause inflammation of the scalp, which can lead to hair loss and damaged follicles.

Inflammation is a process that occurs within the body affecting the white blood cells underneath the scalp. This is called lymphocyte inflammation of the hair follicles. Lymphocytes are white blood cells that are a part of the lymphatic system. When the scalp becomes inflamed, it affects the body internally. Prolonged inflammation can scar hair follicles if not treated properly.

Some ways to reduce inflammation internally include eating dark leafy greens (spinach, chard, kale, and broccoli), fatty fish (sardines, tuna, salmon), whole grains, nuts (almonds, walnuts), peppers, tomatoes, beets, berries (raspberries), and turmeric or ginger. Turmeric supplements can also be taken, although make sure that the supplements are of the highest purity standards and made without fillers. Read the ingredients label to see what other additives or ingredients the supplements contain. Always consult your doctor before trying a new supplement or vitamin.

The key to treating CCCA is reducing inflammation and scalp tissue scarring. Start by removing any tight hairstyles like extensions or weaves. Do not hot comb, relax, or blow-dry your natural hair. You can also reduce inflammation by drinking calendula tea or burdock root tea; both are herbs that help your lymphatic system and swollen lymph glands. You can also use natural ingredients like the ones below in your hair care:

- Manuka honey (with UMF of 10 or higher)
- Raw honey

- Rosemary
- Chamomile
- Calendula
- Chickweed
- Ginger
- Turmeric
- Burdock root
- Aloe vera gel/juice
- Black Soap

You can use the treatments and hair recipes included in this book to reduce inflammation and regrow your hair.

Traction Alopecia

Alopecia is a general term for "hair loss." The word "traction" refers to the pattern of hair loss that can occur in a line across the crown or edges of the scalp. When the hair is under continuous strain from being pulled back tightly or from constricting hair accessories, over time, this can cause hair loss, itchiness, redness, ulcers, and even infections.

Traction alopecia is common among African-American women who have their hair repeatedly styled in tight braids and extensions. Additionally, examples of harmful accessories include tight weave caps and elastic headbands. When natural hair is subjected to discomfort or styled in tight braids or ponytails, high buns, extensions, weaves, or pulled into an updo, the tension causes the scalp to become inflamed. This type of inflammation leads to hair loss.

There are natural hair care treatments for scalp inflammation and thinning edges. For example, castor oil has been promoted as being a possible solution for thinning edges or traction alopecia. Regularly apply castor oil to the affected part of the scalp. Jamaican black castor oil (JBCO) is recommended for this remedy because it undergoes a process that allows many nutrients from the oil to stay intact. You can also add lavender essential oil to the castor oil to increase its potency.

Alopecia Areata

This type of hair loss is characterized by patchy baldness anywhere on the body, so it can also refer to baldness in the beard, eyebrows, eyelashes, armpits, or even inside your nose and ears. Alopecia areata can also happen when the scalp develops an oval or round balding patch. The bald patch can be in the crown of the head. *Alopecia* means "bald skin" and *areata* means "patchy." Alopecia areata is an autoimmune disease, making it different from traction or CCCA alopecia. Cells in the body "attack" hair follicles and cause hair loss.

Female Pattern Baldness

Female pattern baldness, also known in the scientific world as *androgenetic alopecia*, is a type of hair loss caused by continual inflammation of the hair follicle and the conversion of testosterone to the molecule DHT. In females, this type of hair loss creates hair thinning along the crown, in the middle, or back of the scalp. Female pattern baldness is a non-scarring type of alopecia, meaning there is less external damage to the scalp.

When treating any form of hair loss, make sure to consult your doctor before taking any new supplement, herbal treatment, or pharmaceutical drug.

27S Embracing Those in Our Community Who Have Alopecia & Alopecia Remedies

Emotional Healing

Because approximately half of all black women will experience some form or symptom of alopecia in their lifetime, we need to lift our sisters up. Complimenting anyone who wears her hair naturally can brighten her day. Everyone can recall a time when they received a compliment about their hairstyle or headscarf that boosted their self-esteem. That's even more important for those of us with hair loss in a society that idolizes hair. Try connecting on a personal level with others. Many times, we spend most of the day focusing on ourselves. What do I need? What do I want? How can I feel better about myself? However, stepping outside of ourselves to serve and care for other people can help us begin to feel uplifted as well.

See beauty in more than hair. Like the Bible says, "charm is deceptive and physical beauty is fleeting, but a woman who follows the Lord, shall be praised" (Proverbs 31:30 NIV). Give compliments or kind words from the heart. Make sure you are sincere.

Be timely. When you have the chance, don't hesitate. Say it or email it or write it down. However you choose to express your kindness, do it right away. You may never have the moment again to lift someone else up.

Physical Healing from Zinc and Hair Growth for Alopecia Areata

A 2009 study in the *Journal of Annals of Dermatology* shows that patients taking 50 mg daily of zinc were able to recover around 60 percent of hair growth with some being a little less than 60 percent and some being more than 60 percent.

This study was conducted over a twelve-week period with the patients taking the supplements daily and maintained for six months without any other treatment. Patients who had a single alopecia patch showed more improved recovery than those with multiple alopecia patches.

> *According to the study, "Although these patients had a mild type of long-term alopecia areata, zinc supplementation can become a possible adjuvant therapy when combined with other therapeutic methods, and especially for those alopecia areata patients with a low serum zinc level."*

Zinc can be used as a treatment for some forms of hair loss. Zinc supplements have been shown to have a positive impact on hair growth in people with alopecia areata, especially if they already had zinc deficiencies. In fact, according to the study, oral zinc compounds have been used previously to treat different types of hair loss including telogen effluvium and alopecia areata.[1] Always consult your doctor before taking any new supplement, herbal treatment, or pharmaceutical drug.

Natural Treatments and Hair Growth for Alopecia

You can use certain natural ingredients to stimulate hair growth, heal scarring, and reduce inflammation on your scalp.

These ingredients are multi-use and customizable to individual hair routines so you can use them to create a variety of treatments including moisturizing hair masks and scalp massages (massages to specifically stimulate healthy blood circulation and hair growth as well as prevent dandruff). Look for products with these ingredients or feel free to combine them to make your own DIY creamy hair masks and calming sprays.

Ingredients to Look for in Hair Care Products

- Aloe vera gel/juice
- Black soap
- Burdock root tea
- Calendula tea
- Chamomile
- Ginger
- Jamaican black castor oil (JBCO in particular undergoes a process that allows many nutrients from the oil to stay intact. You can also add lavender essential oil to the castor oil to increase its potency.)
- Manuka honey with a UMF of 10 or higher
- Raw honey
- Rosemary
- Turmeric

Essential Oils* for One-Minute Scalp Massages

- Cedarwood
- Clove
- Ginger
- Lemon

- Lemongrass
- Myrrh
- Orange
- Peppermint
- Rosemary
- Sandalwood
- Tangerine
- Tea tree
- Thyme

*Dilute essential oils in a carrier oil like jojoba or argan oil before use.

Recipe: Ginger and Calendula Spray for Inflamed Scalp:

Ingredients
- ⅓ cup ginger, peeled and chopped
- 2 ½ teaspoon calendula flower petals
- ¼ cup aloe vera juice
- ¾ cup water

Instructions
1. Boil ginger and calendula on medium-low for 30 minutes.
2. Strain. The water should be slightly yellow.
3. Add aloe vera juice and water.
4. Pour into a spray bottle and shake.
5. Spray directly on the scalp regularly.

Note: Keep refrigerated for 2–3 weeks. You can substitute fresh rosemary sprigs for the calendula flower petals.

Recipe: Essential Oil Scalp Massage for Hair Growth:

Mix together equal parts jojoba oil and aloe vera gel (the aloe vera gel helps prevent the development of scar tissue on the scalp). Add 2–3 drops of the following essential oils: lavender, cedarwood, thyme, and rosemary. Gently massage mixture onto inflamed scalp 3 times a week. Store in a glass spray bottle. Keep refrigerated for 2–3 weeks. You can substitute grapeseed oil for aloe vera gel to make an oil-only treatment that does not have to be refrigerated.

Recipe: Healing Manuka Honey Hair Mask:

Using a spoon, scoop a tablespoon-size amount of Manuka honey with a minimum rating of 10 UMF into a bowl. Be careful not to dip your fingers into the jar; use a spoon to prevent transference of bacteria. Apply the honey directly to your scalp's affected areas, parting your hair in sections as needed. Gently pat the honey onto your scalp and spread it gently with your fingers. Leave the honey on your scalp for 30 minutes to 1 hour uncovered, then rinse with cool water. Shampoo or style your hair as normal. You can perform this treatment on a weekly or biweekly basis.

Native to Australia and New Zealand, Manuka honey helps to repair skin tissue and ease inflammatory pain on the scalp. The above Manuka hair mask aids in the healing of scalp bumps/sores, eases scalp itching, and provides a temporary protective, antibacterial barrier that promotes wound healing.

28S   Solutions for Scarring Alopecia

Prolonged inflammation, if not treated, can lead to scarring. An inflamed scalp is itchy, red, and can even develop pus and ulcers. To combat scalp inflammation, internal and external routines must be put into place.

Calendula, Burdock Root, and Oils

If the scalp has experienced inflammation or scarring due to CCCA, you can reduce inflammation by drinking calendula or burdock root tea, both of which help to cleanse the lymphatic system and lessen swollen glands. Externally, oils like sea buckthorn oil can be applied to your scalp in a gentle scalp massage to help reduce any scalp scarring.

Omega-3 and Oils

Omega-3 fish oils stimulate the scalp by increasing blood circulation. This can help with naturally regrowing your hair. It can also aid in reducing hair loss associated with inflammation. Externally, oils like chia seed oil are high in Omega-3 and can be applied topically for scalp health.

Turmeric

Turmeric tea or supplements can also help with reducing inflammation due to its anti-inflammatory properties. Be mindful when using turmeric as a supplement because in rare cases, some people are allergic.

More Exercise and Less Technology

Be aware that some inflammation can be due to psychological stressors. Aerobic exercises that increase the heart rate are best for naturally lowering stress levels. Examples of aerobic exercises include:

- Brisk walking
- Jogging or running
- Cycling
- HIIT workouts
- Dancing
- Swimming

Getting enough sleep at night and reducing TV and cell phone use are also ways to reduce chronic stress.

Hair Care Practices

In addition to reducing inflammation, it is also important to avoid hair care routines that will continue to expose the hair and scalp to irritation. In order to avoid irritation:

1. Avoid infrequent washing of the scalp and hair. Always wash your hair at regularly scheduled intervals whether that be every week or every two to three weeks.

2. Use gentle hair products free of chemicals like fragrance/perfume to wash your hair including natural shampoos, conditioners, or deep conditioners.

3. Use a scalp scrub, either homemade or a natural one from the store to naturally scrub your scalp and increase circulation.

29S   *Surgery & Hair Loss*

One of the most difficult forms of hair loss is having your head shaved before surgery or due to cancer treatment. Sometimes after surgery, hair can fall out. This is mainly caused by telogen effluvium. Telogen effluvium is a disruption in the hair follicle growth cycle that impacts its normal routine. Hair loss after surgery is usually temporary.

4 Ways to Cope with Surgery Hair Loss

1. Plan for hair care when you experience hair loss from physical illness first by deepening your worship. Sometimes during extreme brokenness and suffering, we see our frailty and we can identify with Job who arose, tore his robe and shaved his head, and fell to the ground and worshiped his God: "Then Job arose and tore his robe and shaved his head, and he fell to the ground and worshiped. He said, '. . .The LORD gave and the LORD has taken away. Blessed be the name of the LORD.'" (Job 1:20-21, NASB)

2. Remember how God sees you, personally numbers the very hairs of your head (Matthew 10:29-31)—before and after your hair loss. Think of how beautiful you look to others when they see the strength of your faith in the midst of your suffering.

3. Avoid stressors. Be aware that some hair loss after surgery can be due to psychological stressors, which is why aerobic exercises that increase the heart rate are best for naturally lowering stress levels.

4. Third, continue to care for your scalp with your daily hair regimen. Don't give up on your hair growing back!

30S Don't tame the mane.

In hair tutorials, online bloggers will fuss over their baby hairs, using a toothbrush to smooth down their edges into small little waves along their forehead with styling gel. This "taming" of natural curls or kinks is an example of how sleek styles equal beauty and "fuzzy" or "frizzy" hair doesn't. It's part of the larger problem of black women perpetuating false standards of beauty. Who cares if our edges lay flat? And more importantly, why do some think kinky hair is "unfinished?"

I showed a friend a photo of a Bantu knot hairstyle and she preferred the hairstyle when it was taken down and all the waves showed. Bantu knots are a style to be appreciated, as are twists and a twist out.

It's okay to add "finishing touches" to your hair with gel if you want to, but accept the fact that if you didn't and your hair was frizzy and kinky, that's perfectly fine too. Your hair is already finished.

31S *Hair Care for Little Girls*

Sooner or later, you will have to learn how to take care of your hair. It can be a scary thing when no one is around to prompt you with what to do or what to use. In the Oscar-Winning short film *Hair Love*, which is also a children's book by Matthew A. Cherry, who directed the film, viewers follow a little girl as she tries, sometimes comically, but with ever as much grit and determination to style her natural hair. Using a video of her mother, we watch as the little girl tries again and again failing miserably each time to master a particularly complicated hairstyle. It is only later, when her father helps her, that she is able to show off the finished hairdo.

Helping young girls style their own natural hair can be a journey, especially if the parent is not familiar with the proper styling practices. However, it is important to instill in little girls the tenacity and excitement to have their hair styled. We must learn to care for our hair from a young age.

Tips for Creating a Little Girl's Hair Routine

Make it an experience: Let's be real. Hair care is not always fun, even at its best. But it is a necessary component of taking care of yourself. Teach young girls how to set themselves up for success in preparing to style their hair. When it's time to get started, play a favorite song. I recommend "Whip My Hair" by Willow Smith. Set up pillows and cushions to sit on and have a favorite TV show or movie picked out to watch (*The Sea Beast* on Netflix is a good choice). In other words, make hairstyling time an experience she will enjoy. This all helps in building a routine and a positive narrative around styling natural hair.

Use a calendar: Having a calendar, whether digital or physical, that tracks and reminds you of the last time she washed her hair, makes life easier. Instead of spending time trying to guess how long ago her hair was washed or the last time you styled it, a comprehensive calendar can refresh your memory. I recommend adding notes to your calendar such as "Wash Day," "Take-Down Hairstyle Day," or even other helpful reminders like "Deep Condition Today."

Keep it handy: Label a bag or a bucket with the words "Hair Kit" and sit it beside where you usually style hair. Make this your go-to place that keeps all your supplies so that, when you are ready, you can get started right away rather than wasting time looking for that favorite rat tail comb.

Talk it through: A part of teaching is actually conversing about what you are doing when you do it. Good teachers and experienced educators call this a "Think Aloud." As you teach your little girl to style her hair, talk about which products you are using as well as why. Take time to show her the steps in a mirror and talk about each one as though giving a tutorial. This enables her over time to grasp the steps and repeat them when she is ready.

Photograph: Many times we have been told our hair is not manageable and has to be straightened in order to be easier to deal with. Cancel that story. Select new hairstyles to do during styling time by collecting photos online. Keep all the photos in one place and then when it is time to style, let your little girl go to your hairstyle scrapbook to select her next do.

Blog: Sometimes taking pictures of your own unique creations and cataloging them on a blog is the best way to give a self-esteem boost. Let your little girl model at the end of each styling session and photograph the styles. Blog the particulars of the style and the products used to keep track of your hairstyles over the years and what worked well.

Rock it yourself: You know I'm (Sylvia) probably dating myself here when I say "rock it," but really, the best representation of natural hair for your little girl is how you wear your hair. Set the example and your little one will follow your lead.

32S *Stick to the same products.*

When I first started choosing products for my natural hair, I made sure to write down the product name and how well it performed. Keeping up with the best products for your natural hair matters. It's like knowing your favorite brand of chocolate or ice cream. Some things you stick to. Hair products are like that. It's easy to follow the bandwagon of whatever new product comes your way or that is being advertised, but take it from me, in the long run, you will be satisfied you stuck to what worked.

The way to know if a product works is if you are seeing visible results in your hair growth, hair moisture level, and overall hair strength and elasticity (how your hair "bounces" back into place).

My one caveat here is if your products are not showing any results. Or if they are damaging your hair or stunting your hair's growth. If any of your hair products are not helping your hair, it's time to pitch them and move on to something new. Effective hair products make your hair soft, moisturized, somewhat shiny, and easier to detangle and style. Ineffective products do the opposite. Never stick with a brand that's not working for you just because it seems to be working for everyone else.

Admitting Product Addiction

Product junkies live on the need to find the next best product. The underlying desire is to be beautiful. If you're a product junkie, you think that the right product will make your hair look a certain way, and therein lies the problem. The search for this "holy grail" product always continues because you are never satisfied.

You may be a product junkie if you compulsively shop for new products in your free time or if you throw out new products after one use. To avoid becoming a product junkie, you must address the deeper issue underneath the desire to shop. Try answering these questions:

- What do you hope to gain by shopping?
- If you could have the perfect product, what would it look like or do?
- Are you happy with the way your hair looks as it is?

Are you disregarding other products that you already have in order to buy the next big thing? A lot of times, the bigger issue underneath an addiction is a need. Your impulsive buying could be a sign to step back and evaluate your motives.

While there is nothing wrong with casually shopping to buy new products for your hair, you have to set limits. And no matter how many new products you purchase, you won't be happy with the results if you're not already satisfied with yourself and the beauty you have just simply by being you. So don't get caught up in the vortex of "the best is right around the corner" and embrace the beauty you already have.

33S   Product Ingredients to Avoid

Let's talk ingredients. Specifically, which ones to totally avoid. Some of these ingredients can adversely impact your health. And for those of us who like to wash our hair in the shower? Yeah, that means you are actually exposing your *whole* body to these toxic chemicals.

Fragrance: Not All That Smells Well, Ends Well.

Fragrance, otherwise known as aroma or natural flavor, is largely used to add a pleasing scent or taste to cosmetics. For example, fragrances like vanilla or orange flavoring are included in lipsticks to make them taste sweet. Fragrance is usually created by combining synthetic chemicals and it is not regulated by the FDA. That means companies do not have to reveal what chemicals are included in their fragrances. In other words, *any* chemical may be hidden under the word "fragrance" on the ingredient list.

What Makes Fragrance Less Safe

Some fragrances may cause health concerns such as cancer as well as negatively affect the reproductive system by exposure to toxins. Other issues include allergies and skin sensitivities. Fragrance can also contain phthalates, which are linked to possible preterm birth and impaired underdevelopment in girls.[1]

Less is Not More: The Order of Ingredients

Most websites claim to include "featured" ingredients in their cosmetics or they include a glossary of ingredients, explaining the purpose of each component. However, most of the featured ingredients are farther down the ingredient list, which means less of that item is included in the finished product.

To understand an ingredient list, you must start by knowing that the first ingredients listed have a higher percentage in the product while the last items on the list are used at a lower percentage in the product.

A Final Note

Be careful inhaling or sniffing your products. You're better off going with essential oils in your hair products or no fragrance at all. It should be noted that some people are even allergic or sensitive to essential oils. That's when fragrance-free products come especially in handy.

34S Honey, Humectants & Humidity

Honey

When you think of honey, what is the first adjective that comes to mind? Sweet, sticky, creamy, delicious? Sure, honey is a perfect spread for toast and a great sweetener for tea, but what about using honey in your hair care regimen? "Wait, you want me to put that sticky stuff in my hair?!" The answer is a resounding "Yes!" Honey can be very beneficial for your hair! How? Check out some of the facts!

Honey has many restorative and nourishing powers. Honey can add shine and luster to your hair strands. It can also be used to treat baldness or thinning hair. Honey contains natural humectants that allow moisture to lock into curly hair. Humectants also make honey a great conditioner for curly hair. Additionally, honey contains anti-irritant properties. Say goodbye to that dry, sensitive scalp!

Humectants

Humectants draw the moisture from the environment into your hair. Think of humectants as ingredients in products that allow moisture into natural hair similar to how a sponge soaks up water. This can create puffy, frizzy hair on warm days or dry hair on a cold day. These two environments that affect your natural hair are called high humidity and low humidity.

Humidity

High humidity occurs when there is an increased amount of moisture in the air. High humidity usually happens during the summertime or warmer months. The moisture in the air can cause the natural hair to become puffy, frizzy, bloated, and tangled. If you have high porosity hair, avoid humectants as much as possible in order to maintain a healthy hair moisture/protein balance. Humectants can have adverse effects on people with high porosity natural hair (i.e., hair that draws moisture in easily, lets moisture out easily) because the hair becomes puffy or frizzy when too much moisture enters the hair shaft.

Low humidity occurs when there is a low amount of moisture in the air. Low humidity usually happens during the wintertime or colder months. Using a humectant-based product can cause moisture to leave the natural hair. Below are humectants you may find listed in natural hair care products; look for products without chemicals first in the ingredient lists.

Natural humectants:

Honey
Jojoba oil
Shea butter
Aloe vera juice
Vegetable glycerin

Synthetic humectants:

Panthenol
Propylene glycol
Caprylyl glycol

Recommendations & Tips

For premium quality, purchase honey that is grown locally in your state. Try adding honey to deep conditioners, hair masks, and even shampoos for that kick of moisture. Honey can be used with olive oil for a moisturizing scalp treatment.

For a honey pre-poo, combine 1 part honey with ¼ part olive oil. Section hair and apply, leaving on for twenty minutes before rinsing.

35S *Biotin*

Biotin is a vitamin B supplement that helps to maintain healthy hair. Biotin helps strengthen the hair shaft, allowing it to retain length. A deficiency in biotin has been linked to hair loss.[1]

Benefits for Hair

- Generates red blood cells, which improves the flow of blood to the scalp
- Strengthens the hair by providing it with protein
- Helps hair retain length, generates hair growth
- Improves thin, splitting, and brittle hair

Biotin can be found in many foods like nuts, whole grains, meat, fish, and eggs. Did you know that almonds or peanuts are a great source of biotin? Remember to always consult your doctor before taking any type of supplement.

36S Herbs to Know: Thyme, Basil, Ginger & Neem

Let's chit-chat a little bit about each of these herbs and how they can be used for natural hair care.

First up is thyme. Thyme is often labeled as an uncommon essential oil, sidelined for more well-known essential oils like lavender or tea tree. Although overlooked, thyme essential oil is an important oil that can be used medicinally to treat common hair and body ailments.

Thyme is derived from the Greek word *thymos*, which means "to perfume," so it's no wonder that the essential oil is commonly found in perfumes. Beyond being used for its fragrance, thyme essential oil can also be used medicinally to treat hair problems like hair loss and dandruff or other scalp issues.

One study found that thyme, in use with other essential oils, was proven useful in helping those with hair loss from alopecia areata. Participants in the study massaged an oil mix of thyme essential oil, cedarwood essential oil, lavender essential oil, rosemary essential oil, grapeseed oil, and jojoba oil on their scalps in order to improve hair growth.[1]

Another herb to know is sweet basil. Sweet basil is commonly known as a culinary spice used to season Italian dishes like spaghetti; it is also a main ingredient in pesto. Did you know, however, that sweet basil can heal insect bites and stings? Sweet basil's species name, *basilicum*, is derived from Greek and means "kingly" or "royal herb" because it was used as an ingredient in salves for royalty.

Here's another reason why sweet basil is more than just a kitchen spice; it can be used to nourish your hair. Sweet basil naturally moisturizes and adds shine to dull, lackluster hair. It also promotes hair growth and protects your natural hair against breakage. You can use sweet basil in a hair tea rinse or add sweet basil essential oil to your pre-poo treatment or scalp massage. Just add five to six drops to a carrier oil and apply to the scalp.

Along with thyme and sweet basil, we can't forget about ginger. Native to Southeast Asia, particularly China, ginger has natural antioxidant and healing properties. Not only is it helpful in cleansing skin, but combined with calendula, ginger can also be used as a spray to soothe an inflamed scalp; ginger is healing, antiseptic, and anti-inflammatory. This can be helpful for those with scalp irritation from CCCA or traction alopecia.

Finally, neem is a lesser-known herb that is worth learning about. The neem tree (*azadirachta indica*) is native to India and has antibacterial, antifungal, antiseptic, and antiviral properties. The leaves of the neem tree are used to make teas, infusions, and supplements, while the whole nuts of the tree are cold-pressed to make a nourishing oil. Neem can be used both externally and internally to promote the health of skin, hair, and nails.

Due to its antiseptic properties, neem oil can be used to treat scalp ailments like dandruff. Neem oil should first be diluted with a carrier oil (olive oil, coconut oil, etc.) or butter, like shea butter, and then massaged into the scalp to improve blood circulation and slow hair loss.

Since neem is also high in vitamin E, applying neem oil to the skin can produce visible results. Neem oil can aid in healing cracked and dry skin as well as yellowing and brittle nails. What's more, due to its antibacterial and anti-inflammatory properties, applying neem oil topically can help in preventing acne. Neem oil should always be diluted with a carrier oil before using topically. It is important to add that neem oil is for external use only, *not* for consumption.

Neem oil can have a strong smell that may be off-putting to some people. Dilute your neem oil in a carrier oil and add six to ten drops of a strong-smelling essential oil like rosemary or lavender to help with the smell. *Special note: neem should not be used by women who are pregnant.*

37S *Herb to Know: Calendula*

You may have seen calendula listed as an ingredient in your skin products. Not only is this flower a beautiful golden color but it is also known for its skin-healing properties and ability to mend wounds by helping with cell repair and growth.

Calendula for the Skin

Whether applied externally or internally, calendula can aid in preventing infections due to its antiseptic and anti-inflammatory qualities. It is used on the skin in the form of a cream, salve, balm, or ointment to treat bruises, sores, skin ulcers, skin infections, rashes, and even acne. Mothers can use calendula for their babies as it is both soothing and gentle for treating skin problems such as cradle cap, diaper rash, and other common irritations.

To create a balm or salve, dried calendula flower petals must be steeped in olive oil for a minimum of two to four weeks in a dark cabinet or a sunny place. This process is called infusion. After the allotted time, the calendula petals are drained from the olive oil and the oil is now ready to be used in a balm, salve, cream, or ointment.

Calendula for the Body and Hair

Calendula flower petals can also be used to make a nourishing tea. Calendula tea is useful in reducing rising temperatures during a fever. The lymphatic system of the body is also helped by drinking calendula tea; it cleanses and treats swollen glands by removing congestion.

I (Sylvia) use dried calendula to make a delicious tea that can be drunk for those suffering from hair loss due to inflammation. I also use calendula tea in my herbal hair spritz to calm and soothe an inflamed or irritated scalp. Last year, I began growing calendula and loved the results. After harvesting the flowers, I set them to dry and used the flower petals to create my medicinal oil. I steeped the petals in organic olive oil for two to three weeks before removing the petals and using the oil to create balms.

38S   *Herb to Know: Rose Hip*

Rose hips are the seedpods that remain once a rose has shed its petals. A nutrient-rich oil can be extracted from rose hip seeds called rose hip seed oil. This red-orange oil has a high concentration of vitamins C and A and is a lightweight oil that absorbs easily, making it ideal for moisturizing and nourishing hair and skin. Rose hip seed oil can also be helpful in regulating oil secretion in facial skin.

Benefits of Rose Hip Seed Oil for Hair

- Moisturizes hair naturally
- Conditions dry/damaged hair
- Nourishes scalp with vitamin A
- Encourages healthy hair growth
- Makes hair stronger and healthier

Ways to Use Rose Hip Seed Oil

Rose hip seed oil is a fragile oil and must be refrigerated. For your hair, you can use rose hip seed oil in the following ways:

Pre-poo treatment: combine rose hip seed oil with your favorite oil and pre-poo.

Hot oil treatment: include rose hip seed oil in your hot oil treatment mixture.

Deep conditioner: add rose hip seed oil to your favorite deep conditioner.

39S   *Herb to Know: Hibiscus*

Hibiscus tea is a rich, red color and is made by steeping the leaves of the hibiscus plant in hot water. Besides being a beautiful flower, hibiscus can nourish both your body and natural hair.

Hibiscus is native to Angola, which is located on the coast of Southern Africa. It has been used to support cardiovascular health and to lower blood pressure. North Africans in particular have used hibiscus topically to aid in skin health. There are many species of the hibiscus flower, which vary between shades of red, white, pink, and even yellow.

For hair care, hibiscus can be used as a ground powder, infused oil, or tea rinse. For the body, drink hibiscus tea with organic honey or stevia.

Hibiscus Benefits for Hair

- Prevents breakage
- Provides slip to hair
- Strengthens hair shaft
- Soothes dry scalp
- Naturally darkens hair

Recipe: Homemade Hibiscus Tea

Ingredients

    2 cups of water
    2 tea bags of hibiscus tea (organic)
    6 tablespoons of honey (homegrown or organic)

Directions: Boil the water in a tea kettle. Meanwhile, place the two tea bags in a heat-safe Pyrex glass measuring cup. Pour the hot water over the two tea bags and let steep, covered for 3–5 minutes or until the water is a warm red. Remove tea bags carefully. If drinking, add honey to sweeten. If using for hair, do not add honey.

Do It Yourself: Herbal Tea Rinse for Hair

Pour the herb-infused water over your hair, collecting the water in another bowl. Pour the collected water over your hair again. Rinse your hair thoroughly with cold water and style as usual.

40S Recipe: Homemade Flaxseed Gel

A tiny bag of golden flax seeds is basically all you need to make a gel that is ideal for styling mini twists and wash 'n gos, smoothing edges, and sealing the ends of your hair.

What You Need

1 cup of water
Spoon with a long handle
5 ½ tablespoons of flaxseeds
Measuring cup
Measuring spoons
Coffee strainer
Medium-sized pot
4–5 drops of vitamin E oil or tea tree oil

Instructions

Set your coffee strainer right side up into a bowl with a flat bottom. Make sure the coffee strainer is standing, balanced at the bottom of the bowl.

Pour the water into your pot. Turn your stovetop to medium-high heat. Wait for the water to start a low boil. Add your flax seeds one ½ tablespoon at a time while stirring lightly with your spoon.

Turn your stovetop up to high heat. Continue to stir. When the flax seeds begin to secrete a clear mucus, turn off your stovetop. Pour the pot contents into the coffee strainer that is sitting inside the bowl.

The clear mucus should separate itself from the flax seeds and seep through the coffee strainer holes into the bowl. This is your gel.

Wait until all of the gel-like substance has inked through the coffee strainer before removing it from the bowl.

Set the bowl somewhere to cool. Once cooled off, add 4–5 drops of vitamin E oil or tea tree oil as a preservative. Store within your refrigerator when not in use. Gel usually keeps for a week.

41S *Carrier & Essential Oils*

If you have purchased an essential oil before, you may have been instructed to use it with a carrier oil. "Carrier" oil is a term frequently used, but rarely explained. Carrier oils are derived from vegetables, nuts, or seeds. Carrier oils are used in combination with a few drops of an essential oil to avoid irritation and to make the essential oil easier to spread.

Carrier oils that have been cold-pressed or expeller-pressed have not been processed by the use of chemicals. Through the cold-pressed method, oils are obtained by using high pressure to squeeze the plant's leaves or to "crush" the plant's seeds. Cold-pressed carrier oils retain their aroma, vitamins, and nutritional value. Expeller-pressed oils are also obtained by using high pressure, but in addition to this are usually also refined with heat.

Characteristics of Carrier Oils

Oily or slightly oily
Light or strong aromas
Little to no color

What does this mean for your natural hair?

Carrier oils can be used to treat dandruff, soothe an irritated scalp, condition your hair, and to seal in moisture. There is a large variety of carrier oils to choose from, each benefiting your hair in different ways. Depending on the type of oil, some carrier oils can be more expensive than others.

Types of Carrier Oils

Olive oil - $
Coconut oil - $
Grapeseed oil -$
Avocado oil - $$
Sweet almond oil -$
Apricot kernel oil - $
Rose hip seed oil - $$$

Key:

$ = costs around $4 in the United States
$$ = costs more than $4 in the United States
$$$ = costs more than $8 in the United States

Note: Carrier oils can become rancid over time; always check for the expiration date before use.

Ways to Use Carrier Oils for Your Natural Hair

Pre-shampoo treatment (pre-poo)
Scalp massage
Treat dandruff
Condition hair

What Are Essential Oils, Anyways?

Do a simple Google search and you will find many articles speaking about the benefits of essential oils for hair care. But the answer to the question, "What exactly is an essential oil?" is often overlooked. To put it simply, an essential oil is an oil that has been taken from plant leaves, fruits, stems, or roots. Remember, the process of taking the oils from their original source, like plant leaves, is called extraction. Essential oils can be extracted from "exotic" to "everyday" plants. Essential oils can be extracted by using several methods like distillation, expression, solvent extraction, enfleurage, and carbon dioxide extraction. The most common method used to extract essential oils is steam distillation, where the plant is steam cooked in order to release its essences.

Definitions of Essential Oil Extraction Methods

Steam distillation: extracts by steam cooking the plant
Expression: extracts by using high pressure to squeeze the plant
Enfleurage: extracts by saturating the plant with vegetable oils
Carbon dioxide extraction: extracts by using steam from carbon dioxide
Solvent extraction: extracts by using chemicals like alcohol

What Does All of This Mean for Your Hair?

Since essential oils do not feel oily, they can be used to care for natural hair when added to a shampoo, conditioner, pre-shampoo (pre-poo) treatment, hot oil treatment, or when used in a scalp massage.

Characteristics of Essential Oils

Non-oily
Light or strong aromas
Little to no color

How to Use Essential Oils for Natural Hair

Add five to six drops of an essential oil to your favorite shampoo or conditioner for added benefits.

Add five to six drops of an essential oil to the oil(s) in your pre-shampoo or hot oil treatment for added benefits.

Add essential oils to a carrier oil and use it to massage your scalp.

42S *Best Oils for Scalp Massage*

Massaging the scalp can improve the health of your hair and aid in hair growth. Scalp massages increase blood circulation in the scalp, which encourages hair growth. To massage your scalp, use your fingertips to rub in a circular motion on your scalp. Rub your fingertips softly against your scalp clockwise and counterclockwise for one to two minutes at a time. Make sure your nails are cut low so that you do not snag your hair. Only use your fingertips, never your nails, which can scratch and damage your scalp.

Oil for Scalp Massages

When you perform a scalp massage, use a lightweight oil mixed with an essential oil. This mixture will give you the moisturizing benefits of the oils while lessening the chance of clogged pores. The main goal of a scalp massage is not to grease the scalp but to increase the blood circulation to the scalp to aid in hair growth.

Benefits of Scalp Massages

- helps in hair growth
- distributes oil evenly throughout the hair
- increases blood circulation in the scalp
- relieves tension and stress in the scalp

Can I use oil in scalp massages?

Yes, oil is encouraged when performing a scalp massage.

The Best Oils to Use for Scalp Massages

Natural carrier oils are best for scalp massages. Carrier oils are oils that have been cold-pressed or expeller-pressed and have not been processed by the use of chemicals. Carrier oils are used in combination with a few drops of an essential oil in order to avoid irritation and to make the essential oil easier to spread. Some can be found at your local grocery store.

Remember that, because they are concentrated, essential oils should always be diluted by a carrier oil like olive oil, grape seed oil, sweet almond oil, etc. They are also a good option for scalp massages because they have healing effects and strong fragrances that help the scalp and ease stress.

Natural Carrier Oils for Scalp Massages

- Jojoba oil
- Coconut oil
- Grapeseed oil
- Almond oil
- Avocado oil
- Extra virgin olive oil

Essential Oils for Scalp Massages

- Tea tree oil
- Lavender oil
- Eucalyptus oil
- Peppermint oil

Combine three to four drops of an essential oil with a natural carrier oil to create a scalp massage oil mix.

Best Time for Scalp Massage

Great times to perform a scalp massage are in the morning, before bed, and after the hair has been freshly washed. Choose a time that works best for you and massage your scalp daily. In order to benefit from scalp massages, you must be consistent in performing them.

Scalp Massage Oil Mixes/Combinations

Ideal for an oily or irritated scalp

Jojoba oil + tea tree essential oil = nuts and spices fragrance

Ideal for dry scalp or hair that likes oil

Olive oil + eucalyptus essential oil = fresh wintergreen fragrance

Great for an irritated scalp

Grapeseed oil + peppermint essential oil = sweet mint fragrance

Great for dry hair/scalp

Coconut oil + lavender essential oil = Hawaiian island fragrance

43S How to Effectively Use Oil for Your Hair

Oil has pros and cons. One con is an overuse of oil can cause clogged pores. However, using a small amount of oil in your hair care regimen can work great in moisturizing and detangling. When you perform a scalp massage, it is ideal to use a lightweight oil mixed with an essential oil. This mixture will give you the benefits of the oils and lessen the chance of clogged pores. The main goal of a scalp massage is not to grease the scalp but to increase the blood circulation to the scalp to aid in hair growth.

Unfortunately, this may be a hard one for some of us to let go of. You no longer need to be concerned about "greasing your scalp," a phrase that refers to the old practice of applying a cream or oil to the scalp. Instead of greasing your scalp, which can lead to product buildup, try a hot oil treatment on your wash day. To do this, coat your hair with warmed oil (coconut oil works especially well for a pre-shampoo treatment) and place a plastic cap over your hair for fifteen minutes for natural heat. The oil will fortify and nourish your hair as well as prevent shedding and dandruff.

You can also use a small amount of oil to do a pre-poo, style your hair, or lightly moisturize it. How much oil you will use depends on your hair and if it reacts well with oils. I have fine hair, so using oil in a pre-poo works best for me because I can rinse excess oil off of my hair as I wash it. People with thick or coarse hair may prefer using oil to moisturize/style their hair.

Coconut oil is known for effectively penetrating the hair shaft, but the oil that will work best for a pre-poo is up to you. Most oils will penetrate hair strands if heat is applied.

448   Five Ways to Use Olive Oil to Condition Natural Hair

Olive oil is a medium weight oil that is very moisturizing for natural hair with a thick density. Olive oil nourishes both the hair and scalp, preventing dryness and dandruff. Extra virgin olive oil is used in hair care because it is filled with monounsaturated fatty acids and vitamin E, an antioxidant beneficial to the hair.

- Add one tablespoon of olive oil to your favorite deep conditioner recipe to boost the moisture content.
- Use olive oil as a pre-poo treatment: add olive oil to your hair before placing a shower cap on for thirty minutes to one hour.
- Massage olive oil into your scalp as a hot oil treatment after washing your hair.
- Add olive oil to your favorite homemade hair products, butters, and creams.
- Use one tablespoon of olive oil to seal in moisture on wet or damp hair that has been freshly washed.

Do It Yourself: Olive Oil Pre-Poo Treatment

Warm ¼ cup of extra virgin olive oil in a double boiler or for thirty seconds in the microwave. Separate your hair into four to six large twists. Massage olive oil through each twist using your fingertips. Focus on your scalp and hair ends. If you have a small Afro, use your fingertips to massage lightly. Put a shower cap over your head. Wait for thirty minutes to one hour before removing. Wash hair accordingly. For an intense pre-poo, leave the cap on for two to three hours before removing it.

45S Myths That Prevent Us from Wearing Our Natural Hair

Myth #1: "Finding the right products is too hard."

Sorting through an assortment of products can take time, but it is doable. And once you find the right set of products for your hair, the results will be worth the effort. Get to know your hair first, its porosity, texture, and the type of oils or butters it likes. Then look for products with all-natural ingredients. But don't trust the label; read the ingredient list for yourself. Read online articles for product suggestions, but beware of trying to buy everything. Buying all-natural ingredients can sometimes be expensive. Try making your own products as well! Don't be afraid to try something new; we've all had our hair mishaps along the way, but that's what makes it exciting and what leads us to new discoveries that work.

Myth #2: "Men won't think my natural hair is attractive."

There are several issues with this myth. First, no one should love you based solely on physical appearance. It should be your character that matters most. Natural hair *is* attractive, beautiful, and flattering. To say that it is unattractive or that someone would not value you based on how your hair looks is not only problematic but also means that you are devaluing yourself. Look at your natural hair as something you have to offer to the world. Your kinks make you unique, and uniqueness is always something special and meant to be cherished—not changed.

46S   Find a natural hair community.

When you are learning about natural hair, it helps to have community support. Natural hair communities are good for fostering learning, creating friendships, and improving your hair care routine. Join a natural hair community. Choose your favorite hair care blogs, YouTube channels, and websites, and stay connected by commenting and participating in forums.

Our Favorites Are

Love Natural Sunshine (Sylvia's blog)
www.lovenaturalsunshine.co

Natural Hair Rules
www.naturalhairrules.com

Naturally Curly
www.naturallycurly.com

Natural and Proud
www.naturalandproud.com

47S   Finding a Hairstylist

Finding a hairstylist who works with natural hair can be tricky. When looking for a stylist, make sure that they can do natural hair. You're not in need of someone who *thinks* they know how to work with African-American hair. For some stylists, working with African-American hair means just throwing a jar of gel or spraying a can of mousse in your hair to activate the "natural curls." That may work for some, but for others, not so much. Trust me (Sylvia). Been there, tried that, and wasted the money.

I, for one, do not want to visit the salon more than twice a month or every two weeks. This gives me a chance to play with my hairstyle for a while before returning to have a refresh. However, if I was traveling overseas, I may want a hairstyle that can withstand for up to four weeks. That way, I don't have to worry about my hair while not at home. Judging whether a stylist can fit all your hair care needs and lifestyle changes is important.

You can have a highly trained stylist who works well with natural hair and is an expert in various hairstyles, but uses the wrong products for your hair. If your stylist likes to use hair glue, super tight braids, or flat irons regularly, I would look elsewhere. Some hair care practices when used routinely can cause damage to your hair. Search for a stylist that opts for products made with natural ingredients instead and hair care practices that are healthy for the long term.

Wherever your stylist is located, make sure that it is a place that is safe and convenient for you. You want to be able to frequent your hairstylist in comfort, not fight for a spot at the front of the line. Remember: you want to be able to drive there ideally year-round and at early times in the day or on the weekend.

At the end of the day, what matters most is if your natural hair is healthy. Overall, the main thing you want in a stylist is someone who cares about the health of your hair and wants it to grow. Moreover, they should have the expertise and, let's be real, the common sense, to know what will work best for your hair and what will be just plain damaging.

When you select a stylist, you put your trust in their hands and skill sets. My immediate advice is to choose wisely and to never think that you must remain with a stylist to appease them or to help their career or pocketbook. It's your hair and you should be able to entrust it to someone who knows what she or he is doing. When you find a hairstylist who develops that connection with your natural hair, a meaningful bond of appreciation is formed.

48S Natural Hair Q&A

I (Sylvia) wanted to take time to talk about my own personal natural hair journey. We can all learn something by listening to each other's hair stories and building each other up. Let's think of it as a Q&A. Try answering these same questions yourself and then interview a friend or family member who wears her hair naturally. Here are my answers.

Q: What has been the hardest part of your hair journey?

The hardest part of having natural hair was liking it. Don't get me wrong, I love my hair! But sometimes, I would feel like I would get more attention if my hair was straight. Embracing my kinky curls and loving my texture is something I have to remind myself to do daily.

Q: What's your favorite natural hair quote?

"We should look at hair as an art form waiting to be expressed to the world." —Zenobia Jackson

Q: Who is the main person you had to educate about your hair?

I had to educate myself. I did not know how to properly care for my hair. I used to not read ingredient lists on product labels. When I began educating myself about my hair, I was overwhelmed and excited all at once. Today, I believe in using organic or vegan products on my hair. I also enjoy making my own.

Q: What's the best thing you've ever done for your hair?

When I started taking biotin, my hair grew thicker! I have a healthy head of hair because of taking daily vitamin supplements. I also make sure to drink a good amount of water daily. Because I take care of myself from the inside out, my hair has improved.

Q: What's your favorite hairstyle to wear?

I adore the twist out, hands down. It is one of the easiest natural hairstyles to do, and when fluffed out, it looks magnificent. The best part is that no one does their twist outs exactly alike, so there is plenty of room for variety and style.

Q: What's your least favorite DIY natural hair recipe?

I have used molasses as an ingredient in several of my deep conditioners. I have yet to like the results. Molasses makes my hair have a strange "dry cotton" feeling. Instead of using molasses, I now add organic honey or olive oil to my deep conditioners.

GLOSSARY

1B human hair: hair from a donor that has been cleaned, deodorized, processed, and packaged for resale. Hair extensions are labeled by colors starting with the #1. The number one means black and 1B means off-black, which is a more "natural-looking" black for hair extensions. 1B is more sought after in hair extensions because it blends more easily with natural hair.

Alopecia: a general medical term that means "hair loss," specifically any type of hair loss on any part of the body.

Alopecia (CCCA): CCCA alopecia or central centrifugal cicatricial alopecia is when the crown portion of the scalp begins to lose hair in a circular pattern. CCCA alopecia is sometimes called "hot comb" alopecia.

Alopecia (Traction): a type of hair loss caused by pulling the hair too tight. The word "traction" refers to the pattern of hair loss that can occur in a line across the crown or edges of the scalp. Traction alopecia is primarily caused by inflammation of the scalp.

Alopecia (Androgenetic): Female pattern baldness, also known in the scientific world as androgenetic alopecia, is a type of hair loss caused by continual inflammation of the hair follicle and the conversion of testosterone to the molecule DHT. In females, this type of hair loss creates hair thinning along the crown or in the middle or back of the scalp. Female pattern baldness is a non-scarring type of alopecia, meaning there is less external damage to the scalp.

Bantu knots: Bantu knots involve wrapping a single strand of hair around itself. Bantu knots also work on natural or curly hair with a defined curl pattern.

Bantu knot outs: strands of hair that are twirled and wrapped in a circular motion and later unwrapped to create a loose, somewhat springy hair texture. A Bantu Knot Out is a hairstyle that creates springy waves in natural and curly hair. They are ideal for "kinky hot hair" (also known as 4c) as they create a coiled look on hair that does not have a prominent curl pattern when dry.

Butters: solid fatty substances used in hair care to lock in moisture and prevent the hair shaft and end of hair from drying. Butters can be combined by melting with a double boiler or mixing together in a conventional kitchen mixer with oils to make whipped butter that is easier to spread. Butters like shea and cocoa butter are extracted from nuts and are natural. Other examples of natural butters include kokum, mango, Tucuma, Murumuru, and Cupuacu butters. Unnatural butters, which do not occur naturally in nature, are actually a blend of hydrogenated soybean oil and other oils to create a substance that resembles a whipped buttercream.

Buzz cut: shaving hair as low as possible to the scalp.

Cold perms: a chemical process that alters the keratin (proteins in your hair). Cold perms, also known as alkaline perms, work quicker and contain the chemical ammonium thioglycolate. Perms differ from relaxers, which are white lotions (also known as "creamy crack") that straighten Afro-textured hair.

Cornrows: the interlocking and crisscrossing of three strands of hair to braid it in sections close to the scalp. Braids are usually divided into even rows and can include extensions for length.

Cowash: conditioning your hair by using a conditioner to "clean" the hair instead of a shampoo, which can be helpful after playing sports or swimming in chlorinated water. This is a lighter way to "wash" the hair between regular washes, but this method should not be used to replace shampooing altogether.

Creams: water-based moisturizers for hair, usually white and solid, that resemble a lotion and are easily absorbed. Creams are used to hydrate dry hair and are used in the last step of the "LOC" method to lock in moisture to the hair. Creams can vary from light to heavy, depending on the oils included.

Crochet hair: Extensions that include loops and can be "crocheted" into cornrows using a crochet hook method to create a seamless look that makes the fake hair appear to grow directly out of the scalp. Crochet hair can include locs, curls, and braids.

Extensions: classified as anything that is added to the hair to create length or the illusion of another style. Extensions commonly include straight braiding hair that is either synthetic (man-made materials/fibers) or human (real hair that has been sanitized and commercially packaged to be sold) and can be dyed in various colors. Extensions can also include crochet weave and clip-ins (similar to tracks of weave with open/close comb-like "clips" that allow the hair to be added).

Emollients: Emollients are oils or synthetic chemicals that are used to provide sheen, prevent moisture loss, and soften the hair. Natural emollients, like oils, are best to use in hair care because they are less likely to cause irritation, fizziness, and product buildup. While synthetic emollients hide the damage hair strands may have suffered by covering the hair, natural emollients nourish the hair over time.

Fairy knots: small knots that form at the end or midpoint of individual strands of hair, creating a point for breakage to occur.

Gel: a sticky, gelatinous styling product similar in texture to jelly used to flatten and smooth down edges (also known as "baby hairs") or other parts of the hair. Usually used with a toothbrush to brush hair along the hairline.

Havana twist: Havana twists are large, kinky twists created by using Havana hair extensions. Havana hair is textured, synthetic hair extensions. Havana hair is made to look similar to kinky, natural hair, or Marley hair extensions. Havana hair is lightweight and can be styled in buns, ponytails, or left to hang.

Hot combs: straightening tools that are heavy iron combs that are heated commonly on a stove in the kitchen and then combed through kinky hair to straighten it. Hot combs can cause burn marks on the forehead or the neck if used too close to the skin.

Human hair wigs, pieces, etc.: Human hair is exactly what it sounds like, hair that used to live on a donor's head. The real hair is cut, cleaned, or processed so that it can be packaged and sold in beauty stores as wigs. Wigs and other hair pieces/extensions made from human hair are largely preferred because they appear more realistic and do not mat as easily and can have more longevity.

Humectants: Humectants draw moisture from the environment into your hair. This can create puffy, frizzy hair on a warm day or dry hair on a cold day. These two environments that affect your natural hair are called high humidity and low humidity.

Jheri curl: a curly relaxer of sorts that changes the texture of kinky hair so that it is curly. Jheri curl styles were very popular in the late 80s and 90s. The Jheri curl has to stay very moisturized to prevent breakage, usually by spraying it to drench it with hydration.

LOC/LCO: The LOC Method refers to the order in which you apply three products—liquid, cream, and oil in order to moisturize your natural hair. You can remember the sequence to use these products by the order of the letters. The "L" stands for liquid, the "C" for cream, and the "O" for oil. The LCO Method differs from the commonly known LOC Method because of the order in which the products are used. Both methods are used to moisturize natural hair so that it stays hydrated longer.

Locs: the specific method of twisting kinky hair and leaving it to "lock" around itself creating a "loc." Think Bob Marley. However, locs can be cut, shaped, and styled to fit the wearer. They can be worn long or short as well as dyed. Locs require routine appointments with a licensed loctician to both initially style the hair and maintain it. Loc styles include traditional and sisterlocks, to name a few.

Lye relaxers: the original way of chemically straightening kinky hair, dating back as far as the '50s and 60s. The lye burns the scalp, but it is largely believed that the longer the cream is in, the more "straight" your hair will become. Lye relaxers are very damaging to both hair and scalp over time and can cause hair loss.

Micro braids: skinny braids that are created by using small sections of hair. Micro braids usually result in having a lot of braids with the ends of the hair left unbraided to hang straight. Micro braids can be manipulated into a variety of styles including buns and ponytails.

Moisturizers: the curl pattern of kinky hair prevents it from easily transferring and distributing the natural oils from the scalp throughout the hair strands. Therefore, moisturizers like creams are needed to hydrate the hair. Moisturizers are commonly sold in bottles or jars and the first ingredient is water or aloe vera juice for maximum nourishment.

No visible scarring hair implants: follicular unit extraction (FUE). For natural hair in African-American women, the FUE is the preferred type of hair transplant. Hair transplant procedures depend on your hair type, color, and even the area in which you are having new hairs placed. Placing new hairs into the scalp is called "grafting." The hair transplant process is when the doctor takes the grafts, which hold individual hair follicles, and uses a needle or scalpel to delicately place each graft into the scalp. Hair transplants can take anywhere between four to eight hours. More can be added for even thicker hair.

Perm rods: hard, plastic rollers that come with an elastic spring that holds the hair in place after it has been rolled. Used to style hair in curls that are bigger, curlier, and more widely accepted as less kinky.

Pomade: a sticky substance, usually wax-based used to smooth hair or to create a sealant over the hair shaft to lock in or to help retain moisture. Pomades can sometimes be applied to the scalp in a method called "greasing the scalp," but this is not recommended as excessive use of pomades can clog pores.

Porosity: how hair absorbs moisture into the hair strand. If the hair has been damaged from dying or perms/relaxers, it can easily absorb moisture but have trouble retaining that hydration, leading to dry or brittle hair. Porosity ranges from low porosity to high porosity, which specifies if the hair cuticle is raised or lowered. With low-porosity hair, the hair cuticle is too closed, which makes it difficult to get moisture into the hair. In high porosity, the hair cuticle is too open, allowing moisture in easily, but at the same time easily losing moisture as well. This can create puffy and dry hair. Healthy hair has the ideal moisture absorption and retention capabilities, does not become dry easily, and has elasticity and sheen.

Pre-condition: the process of applying a conditioner to the hair before washing. This can include using the pre-poo process or using a commercial conditioner to moisturize the hair before washing. Pre-condition can help hair retain moisture and can prevent hair from becoming dry or stripped of its hydration during a cleaning.

Pre-poo: the process of moisturizing hair before shampooing. A pre-poo is the abbreviation of the word pre-shampoo. A pre-shampoo is a treatment applied to the hair before shampooing/washing. Pre-poo treatments can be done with oil or with a conditioner. An example of an oil that works well for pre-poo treatments is coconut oil. To pre-poo, section hair and apply oil or conditioner from root to tip. Place a plastic shower cap over the hair for 30 min. Shampoo/wash hair as usual.

Protective hairstyles: hairstyles that give your actual hair a rest from constant daily or weekly styling. Protective hairstyles are low manipulation. In other words, it keeps your hands out of your hair. Some examples are weaves, wigs, and extensions like twists and braids, as well as crochet extensions. When done properly, without being too tight or without being left in too long, protective hairstyles can give your hair a much-needed break and allow it to strive while you do life.

Sealants: these are the butters and oils you use on your hair after a leave-in conditioner to "seal" in the moisture by flattening the hair cuticle. Each strand of hair is made up of layers that are damaged over time due to styling practices or the weather. This process is called a raised cuticle and sometimes it looks like dry, frizzy hair. Sealants help the hair's cuticle lay flat, keeping the hair hydrated and less susceptible to breakage.

Sew-in weave: this process is done when the hair is parted and braided in rows and then the hair is attached using a needle and thread to sew the "weave tracks" into the braids. Weave tracks are hair that is attached to long ribbon-like threads and divided into separate pieces to be sewn into the hair. Some stylists choose to glue in weave tracks instead.

Skinny twists: twists that are smaller in size than regular twists. Synthetic hair can be added in different colors to create a bob of twists.

Surgical hair implants: Hair transplants are when hair follicles are taken from another area of the scalp, preferably the back, and moved to the thinning areas of the scalp to re-grow. There are two types of hair transplants: follicular unit strip surgery (FUSS) or follicular unit extraction (FUE). For natural hair in African-American women, the FUE is the preferred type of hair transplant. Hair transplant procedures depend on your hair type, color, and even the area in which you are having new hairs placed. Placing new hairs into the scalp is called "grafting."

Synthetic hair: Also known as fake hair, this is the hair that is sold in packs in beauty salons for braids and twist extensions. Synthetic hair does not come from a human donor and is created from man-made fibers. It is usually a lot cheaper, comes in a variety of colors including neons, and can be used in braids that are burned at the ends with a lighter to keep from unraveling.

TWA (teeny-weeny Afro): an acronym for a small Afro that is common to women who have a "big chop."

Twist out: the go-to style for most women with kinky hair that involves parting the hair into sections and then styling it by interlocking two strands of hair in a twist motion. Twists can be left overnight under a satin bonnet and then untwisted in the morning to create a kinky, curly hairstyle. Looks like a texturized Afro.

Twist-and-snip method: a way to tame split ends by styling kinky hair in twists and then using shears to cut the ends of the hair.

Twists: parting the hair into sections and then styling it by interlocking two strands of hair in a twist motion.

Un-gelled edges: also known as "baby hairs," these are the parts of your hair nearest to your forehead that are sometimes viewed as frizzy or unkempt. Not choosing to put gel on your edges means your hair is free to do what it wants. It's both liberating and scary, but there is freedom in not having to brush your hair edges down to look slick and straight because who said straight, smooth edges were beautiful and un-gelled edges were unruly?

ACKNOWLEDGMENTS

First and foremost, I want to acknowledge my faith in God for it is because of the Lord that I am who I am, and I am all that he wants me to be.

I want to acknowledge my wonderful parents, Ethel Lee (affectionately called Madear), heavenward in 2007, and Johnny B. (lovingly called Daddy), heavenward in 2011, who always believed in me and who were my first heroes.

It is with deepest thanks I acknowledge the following special people in my life:

To my handsome husband, **Donald**, the love of my life who is always my champion, my defender, and my closest confidant.

To our lovely daughters, **Melissa and Sylvia**, who are such talented, awesome, godly women of character and my closest girlfriends and whom I am honored to be on this writing team with.

To our remarkable son, **Donald Anthony**, who is in his own right a creative visionary and artistic writer and our lovely, talented daughter-in-law, **Debbie**.

To all my siblings and family members: my hero sister, **Janice**, my prolific poet youngest brother, **Douglas**, and my big brother, the doctor minister **Marvin**. To all my wonderful sister-in-laws, especially **Michelle** and **Carol** and all my sweet nephews and nieces especially **Janelle** and **Karla**. To my beautiful aunties **Ruth, Ann, Mildred, Bobbie**, and **Aunt Mae** along with my uncles and host of cousins.

To all my dear friends who have stuck with me through the years: **Gail** (my closest childhood friend), **Leah, Carolyn, Paula, Maria, and Kamia** as well as to all my close prayer warrior sisters and Soror sisters who never grew weary in praying for me and supporting me.

Shelia Burlock

The three of us want to especially thank our publisher, Senior Editor, and friend, **Adrienne Ingrum**, whom when we first met her, was like an angel with a halo of gorgeous silver natural hair. It is because of her belief and all she did to invest in us as first-time authors that this book has become a reality.

It takes a village to bring a book into the world and we are so grateful to the one we have at Broadleaf Books, including: Alyssa and the rest of the publicity & marketing team, Erin, Carlos, and Andrew. Thank you all for your passionate work, and also Diedre, our copy editor.

**Shelia Burlock, Sylvia Burlock,
and Melissa Burlock**

A Brief Timeline of Black Hair

1400S–2000S

1400s

In Africa, elaborate hairstyles were an unspoken language. They told observers the wearer's identity, such as the person's social and marital status, religious affiliation, ethnicity, surname, age, and kingdom citizenship. Different hair sculptures were so complicated that they required days to complete.

African men and women use hairdressing recipes and tools, like decorative wide-tooth combs, to maintain the health of their hair. Shea butter, coconut oil, and black soap are widely used to style and wash hair. African women wear cornrows with complex patterns that reflect the mathematical concepts of fractals and infinity.

Mangbetu women wear edamburu hairstyles by arranging their braids in a cylindrical design that ends in a halo-like disc.

Fulani women wear fan-shaped crest hairstyles, while young men wear their hair in braids wrapped in gold.

Masai women shave their heads and wear ornate jewelry, while men who are warriors plait their hair in hundreds of threadlike twists.

Egyptians wear wigs dyed black for daily wear and different colors for ceremonial occasions.

Humbi women wear beaded hairstyles shaped similarly to ceremonial wigs used in Egypt.

In Sub-Sahara Africa, women wear three-dimensional threaded hairstyles. The technique of hair threading, which is achieved by wrapping black thread around hair sectioned in patterns, later evolves in Southern Nigeria, where women develop a variety of threaded hairstyles.

1500s–1800s

During the transatlantic slave trade and enslavement, white enslavers denigrate the natural hair texture of African and African-descendant peoples as subhuman "wool" and hack off enslaved people's hair as a means of psychological and physical violence.

White traders shave the heads of newly kidnapped and enslaved African persons. This act of violence is perpetrated in an attempt to both humiliate the men and women and sever their cultural ties to the identities the hairstyles symbolized in their own communities.

White plantation masters and mistresses fabricate the dichotomy of "good" (i.e., European or straight) hair versus "bad" (i.e., Afro-textured or black hair) in order to enforce white supremacy.

White plantation mistresses in particular perpetrate the act of cutting off hair as a form of punishment against enslaved black women.

In an act of resistance, enslaved black women style their hair in cornrows to encode messages, create "maps" to freedom, and even hide seeds.

1900–1950s

By the twentieth century, African Americans have survived centuries of enslavement and a Civil War. They were free, albeit within a racist society. Through adopting Eurocentric standards for personal style, like straightened hair, black people sought to assimilate into white-dominant spaces and thereby improve their social standing and livelihood. Elite and middle-class blacks prize straight hair and light skin as markers of an elevated status, perpetuating the same hierarchy of physical traits that originated with slavery. As the black middle class grew so did the black beauty market, which became defined by two of the country's first self-made female millionaires.

In 1902, Annie Minerva Turnbo Malone (1869–1957), chemist, philanthropist, beauty entrepreneur, and the daughter of formerly enslaved parents, relocates her black hair care business from Illinois to St. Louis, Missouri. One of the country's first self-made female millionaires, Malone establishes her cosmetology school, Poro College, in 1918.

Madame C. J. Walker (1867–1919), also the daughter of formerly enslaved parents and a former employee of Malone's, launches Madam Walker's Wonderful Hair Grower, her own line of black hair care products, in 1906. Walker's brand is a national and international sensation, and she becomes the most famous self-made female millionaire in American history.

1960s

The Civil Rights Movement marks the beginning of the natural hair movement and African Americans' celebration of their Afro-textured hair.

The Supremes (Diana Ross, Mary Wilson, and Florence Ballard) wear voluminous bouffant wigs. Jimi Hendrix and The Jackson 5 sport Afros.

Cicely Tyson debuts cornrows on *East Side/West Side* (1963), becoming the first black woman to wear the natural hairstyle on national television. Nichelle Nichols stars as Lt. Uhura in *Star Trek*, becoming the first black woman to star in a leading TV role. Diahann Carroll stars in *Julia*.

Ebony and *Jet* magazines, founded by John H. Johnson in 1945 and 1951 respectively, showcase positive images of natural hair textures while chronicling societal issues defining the 1960s by spotlighting black civil rights leaders, protesters, and black celebrities in sports, music, fashion, film, and TV. The publications popularize hairstyles worn by black models and new products for black hair.

Essence magazine is founded by four black entrepreneurs in 1968 as the first lifestyle publication to center African-American women. It launches its first issue in May 1970.

1970s–1980s

Growing out of the Civil Rights Movement, the Black Power Movement encourages Black people to embrace their natural hair as beautiful.

Black Power Movement leader Angela Davis's iconic Afro symbolizes cultural pride and the rejection of Eurocentric beauty standards.

Chaka Khan wears big hair that rocks just as hard as her voice; Donna Summer wears luscious locks; Nina Simone switches from straight hairdos to Afrocentric hairstyles; and the groundbreaking TV show *Soul Train* debuts in 1971, spotlighting black music, dance, and hair.

 Nikki Giovanni and Toni Morrison publish their debut titles in 1968 and 1970, respectively. They both wear their natural hair in Afros.

 Willie Lee Morrow (1939–2022) publishes *400 Years Without a Comb* in 1973, chronicling black hairstyling practices from Africa through enslavement to the 1960s. Morrow was a barber, inventor, and entrepreneur who developed the predecessor to the Jheri curl and popularized the use of the Afro pick among African Americans.

 Actors in *Good Times* and *The Jeffersons* wear their natural hair. The Afroed blaxploitation film icon Pam Grier stars in *Foxy Brown* (1974). The Jheri curl becomes popular, taking center stage in Michael Jackson's music video for "Thriller" (1982) and *Coming to America* (1988). Characters in Spike Lee's *School Daze* (1988) wear different black hairstyles.

1990s

 From Brandy's micro braids to the curly hairdos of Tia and Tamera Mowry, hairstyles like twists, braids, and wigs are represented in popular black sitcoms like *Moesha*, *Sister Sister*, and *Living Single*.

 Janet Jackson popularizes long box braids after debuting the style in her 1993 movie, *Poetic Justice*. In 1997, Brandy stars in *Cinderella* as the titular Disney princess wearing her micro braids.

With her signature buzz cut, the model and designer Alek Wek becomes the first African woman and the first black woman to be featured on the cover of *Elle Magazine* in November 1997.

Erykah Badu dons a head wrap on the cover of her debut album *Baduizm* (1997) and wears a shaved head to the 2001 Grammys. Lauryn Hill appears on the cover of the 1999 "World Most Beautiful" issue of *People* magazine wearing dreadlocks, a year after the release of her debut solo album, *The Miseducation of Lauryn Hill*.

Venus and Serena Williams, wearing their hair in twin beaded styles, explode onto the elite tennis scene in the 1990s and change the game forever.

2000s

Natural hair blogs like Afrobella, Curly Nikki, Naptural85, and Urban Bush Babes revitalize the Afro hair movements of the 1960s and 1970s, popularizing hairstyles like cornrows, weaves, crochet braids, wigs, and wash-and-gos. Discrimination against black hairstyles is met with fearless resistance and fierce political change.

Natural hair anthems premiere including: "I Am Not My Hair" by India.Arie (2006); "Whip My Hair" by Willow Smith (2010); and "Don't Touch My Hair" by Solange Knowles (2016).

During the 2012 Olympics, Gabby Douglas is trolled online for her hair. In September 2020, the gold medalist shows off her natural hair in an Instagram post and reveals her experience with traction alopecia.

After an entertainment reporter makes a racist comment about Zendaya's dreadlocks during the 2015 Oscars red carpet, the actress and singer deftly responds in an Instagram post validating the beauty and professionalism of the hairstyle.

Forever First Lady Michelle Obama starts wearing her natural hair for the first time since leaving the White House in 2017. She has reportedly said Americans "weren't ready" for a first lady with natural hair.

Films and TV shows premiere directed by and/or featuring black men, women, and children wearing a diverse array of natural hairstyles, including: *Black-ish* (2014), *Insecure* (2016), *Black Panther* (2018), *Nappily Ever After* (2018), *Jingle Jangle: A Christmas Journey* (2020), *Woman King* (2022), *Obi-Wan Kenobi* (2022), and *Queen Charlotte: A Bridgerton Story* (2023). In April 2023, Halle Bailey stars as the Disney Princess Ariel in *The Little Mermaid* with bright red dreadlocks.

Sparked by racist incidents like a white referee forcing high schooler Andrew Johnson to have his dreadlocks publicly sheared, the Creating a Respectful and Open World for Natural Hair (CROWN) Act passes the House of Representatives in March 2022, prohibiting discrimination based on one's hair texture or hairstyle.

Sporting shoulder-length sisterlocks, Judge Ketanji Brown Jackson becomes the first Black woman and the 116th Associate Justice to be appointed to the US Supreme Court in 2022.

NOTES

Introduction: New Growth

1. *Nomadic women of Chad believe God left Chébé in the mountains to use in their ancient hair-care practices*: Lauren Valenti, "The Thousand-Year-Old Hair Ritual That's Alive and Well in Chad." *Vogue*, March 8, 2022, https://www.vogue.com/article/chebe-hair-ritual-chad.

Hairmeneutics

1. *Hermeneutics*: "Hermeneutic," *Merriam-Webster.com*, accessed May 3, 2023, https://www.merriam-webster.com/dictionary/hermeneutic.

Melissa's Hair Story: Tresses & Stresses

1. *Black beauty shops are predominantly owned by Korean Americans*: Michael Corkery, "A Korean Store Owner. A Black Employee. A Tense Neighborhood," *New York Times*, October 15, 2020, https://www.nytimes.com/2020/10/15/business/beauty-store-race-protests.html?auth=register-email&register=email; Emma Sapong, "Roots of Tension: Race, Hair, Competition and Black beauty stores," *MPR News*, April 25, 2017, https://www.mprnews.org/story/2017/04/25/black-beauty-shops-korean-suppliers-roots-of-tension-mn.

2. *CCCA destroys hair follicles*: Paula Ludmann, "Hair Loss Types: Central Centrifugal Cicatricial Alopecia Overview," *American Academy of Dermatology Association*, March 14, 2022, https://www.aad.org/public/diseases/hair-loss/types/ccca; Crystal Aguh and Amy McMichael, "Central Centrifugal Cicatricial Alopecia," *JAMA Dermatology* 156, 9 (2020): 1036. https://doi.org/10.1001/jamadermatol.2020.1859; Candrice R. Heath, Caroline N. Robinson,

and Roopal V. Kundu, "Central Centrifugal Cicatricial Alopecia (CCCA)," *Skin of Color Society*, https://skinofcolorsociety.org/patient-dermatology-education/central-centrifugal-cicatricial-alopecia-ccca/.

3.   *Black women's hair is 2.5x more likely to be perceived as unprofessional:* JOY Collective and Modulize on behalf of Dove and LinkedIn, *2023 CROWN Research Study*, https://www.thecrownact.com/research-studies.

4.   *Black women are more likely to change their hair for the workplace:* JOY Collective, *The CROWN Research Study (2019)*, https://www.thecrownact.com/research-studies.

5.   *Female pattern baldness hair loss is typically concentrated on the top of my head and in the crown:* Jessica Migala, "Male vs. Female Pattern Baldness (Androgenetic Alopecia): What's the Difference?" *Everyday Health*, December 15, 2022, https://www.everydayhealth.com/hair-loss/male-vs-female-pattern-baldness-androgenetic-alopecia/.

Spiritual & Historical Roots

1.   *Among Yoruba people and Yoruba spiritualty, hairstyles have great meaning:* Ayana Byrd and Lori Tharps, *Hair Story: Untangling the Roots of Black Hair in America* (St. Martin's Griffin, 2014), 4.

2.   *Long hair is linked to spiritual energy and cultural identity:* "Women From Three Faith Communities Share How Their Long Hair and Spirituality Are Connected," *Allure*, May 17, 2018, https://www.allure.com/story/long-hair-and-religious-spirituality-connection.

3.   *Hairstyles communicated aspects of a person's identity in various kingdoms:* Byrd and Tharps, *Hair Story*, 2.

4.   *Hairstyles change with the stages of a woman's life:* Oreoritse Tariemi, "Otjize: The Red Beauty Miracle of The Himba People," *Guardian Life*, January 27, 2022, https://guardian.ng/life/otjize-the-red-beauty-miracle-of-the-himba-people/.

5. *Enslaved black women mixed household ingredients together to style their natural hair or meet Eurocentric beauty standards*: Byrd and Tharps, *Hair Story*, 17.

6. *Uterine cancer affects black women more than women of other races*: Che-Jung Chang, Katie M. O'Brien, Alexander P. Keil, Symielle A. Gaston, Chandra L. Jackson, Dale P. Sandler, and Alexandra J. White, "Use of Straighteners and Other Hair Products and Incident Uterine Cancer," *JNCI: Journal of the National Cancer Institute* 114, 12 (December 2022): 1636–1645, https://doi.org/10.1093/jnci/djac165; Becky Sullivan, "Hair Straightening Chemicals May Increase Women's Risk of Uterine Cancer, Study Finds," *NPR*, October 19, 2022, https://www.npr.org/2022/10/19/1129764003/hair-straightening-chemicals-may-increase-womens-risk-of-uterine-cancer-study-fi.

7. *Black women spend millions on hair care*: Nelly Ghansah, "The Afro Tax: African American Women Spend Four Times More on Hair Care Than Caucasian Women," *The AFRO*, April 11, 2023, https://afro.com/the-afro-tax-african-american-women-spend-four-times-more-on-hair-care-than-caucasian-women/.

Hair Identity

1. *The forced removal of Andrew Johnson's dreadlocks elicited national outrage and new legislation*: Jesse Washington, "The Untold Story of Wrestler Andrew Johnson's Dreadlocks: How the High School Athlete Endured His Infamous Haircut," *Andscape*, September 18, 2019, https://andscape.com/features/the-untold-story-of-wrestler-andrew-johnsons-dreadlocks/.

2. *Nazir*: "H5139—nāzîr—Strong's Hebrew Lexicon (nlt)," *Blue Letter Bible*, accessed May 4, 2023, https://www.blueletterbible.org/lexicon/h5139/nlt/wlc/0-1/.

3. *The CROWN Act prohibits hairstyle or hair texture discrimination*: Rose Minutaglio, "The Crown Act Banning Discrimination Against Natural Hair Was Passed by the House," *Elle*, March 18, 2022, https://www.elle.com/beauty/a31400745/the-crown-act-

what-to-know/; Black Information Network, "CROWN Day: Everything You Need To Know About The Celebration Of Black Hair," July 1, 2022, *Chicago Defender*, https://chicagodefender.com/crown-day-everything-you-need-to-know-about-the-celebration-of-black-hair/.

In Touch with My Hair

1. *Enslaved black women covered their hair out of necessity:* Byrd and Tharps, *Hair Story*, 12–13; Willie L. Morrow, *400 Years Without a Comb* (Willie Lee Morrow, 1973), 25.

God honors my hair.

1. *Enslaved people's hair was described as "wool" by their enslavers:* Shane White and Graham White, "Slave Hair and African American Culture in the Eighteenth and Nineteenth Centuries," *Journal of Southern History* 61, 1 (February 1995): 56, https://www.jstor.org/stable/2211360.

God has already anointed my head.

1. *People traditionally used oil to anoint each other and receive God's blessings:* Kyle Blevins, "What Does It Mean To Be Anointed?" *Crosswalk*, April 19, 2022, https://www.crosswalk.com/faith/bible-study/what-does-it-mean-to-be-anointed.html.

The Black Hair Community

1. *Among African societies, hairdressers were examples of spiritual advancement:* Byrd and Tharps, *Hair Story*, 5.

Black Hair in Church

1. *Black women would share hair information with each other in church:* Byrd and Tharps, *Hair Story*, 16.

I surrender all.

1. *Nāzîr:* "H5139 - nāzîr - Strong's Hebrew Lexicon (nlt)," *Blue Letter Bible*, accessed May 4, 2023, https://www.blueletterbible.org/lexicon/h5139/nlt/wlc/0-1/.
2. *Nazirite:* W. Christie, "Nazirite—International Standard Bible Encyclopaedia," *Blue Letter Bible*, last modified May 5, 2003, https://www.blueletterbible.org/search/Dictionary/viewTopic.cfm.

Grief & Alopecia

1. *Dr. Elisabeth Kübler-Ross first described the five stages of grief in her 1969 book On Death and Dying:* Elisabeth Kübler-Ross, *On Death and Dying* (Scribner, 1969).
2. *The stress of bereavement can cause allopecia:* Pirie Jones Grossman, "Jocelyn Jackson Williams of MBJ Consulting: 5 Things You Need to Heal After a Dramatic Loss or Life Change," April 25, 2021, https://medium.com/authority-magazine/jocelyn-jackson-williams-of-mbj-consulting-5-things-you-need-to-heal-after-a-dramatic-loss-or-93a510e47b97.

Don't be a long hair hater.

1. *Covering one's hair while praying has been a historical cultural-historical practice:* John F. Walvoord and Roy B. Zuck, *The Bible Knowledge Commentary: An Exposition of the Scriptures by Dallas Seminary Faculty (New Testament Edition)* (Victor Books, 1986), 530.

Protection is perfection.

1. *Black children experience hair discrimination early:* JOY Collective on Behalf of Dove, "2021 CROWN Research Study for Girls Finds 53% of Black Mothers Say Their Child Experienced Hair Discrimination As Early As 5 Years Old," *PR Newswire*, January 26, 2022. https://www.thecrownact.com/all-press/ebonycom/style/beauty/dove-early-as-five-hair-discrimination-film-9hstp.

What is natural?

1. *Each black person's crown of hair is unique:* Morrow, *400 Years Without a Comb*, 54.

It's all about the scalp.

1. *Calendula heals the body:* Rosemary Gladstar, *Rosemary Gladstar's Herbal Recipes for Vibrant Health* (Storey Publishing, 2008), 318.

Swim Day

1. *There is now an Olympic-approved swim cap for black hair:* Marina Pitofsky, "Soul Cap, a Swimming Cap Designed for Black hair, Approved After Ban from the Olympics," *USA Today*, September 8, 2022, https://www.usatoday.com/story/sports/olympics/2022/09/07/soul-cap-black-hair-tokyo-olympics/8014200001/.

Being about Head Wraps

1. *After Emancipation, straight and textured hair evoked perceptions of social class:* Byrd and Tharps, *Hair Story*, 13; 152.
2. *Black women wore headscarves as an act of defiance:* Samantha Callender, "The Tignon Laws Set the Precedent for the Appropriation and Misconception Around Black Hair," *Essence*, October 24, 2020, https://www.essence.com/hair/tignon-laws-cultural-appropriation-black-natural-hair/.

Superior Ways to Moisturize Natural Hair Year-Round

1. *Drink at least four to six cups of water everyday:* Howard E. LeWine, "Review of "How much water should you drink?" *Harvard Health Publishing*, https://www.health.harvard.edu/staying-healthy/how-much-water-should-you-drink.

Alopecia

1. *The chance of hair loss increases with age:* Devon Abelman, "I Lost My Hair in My 20s," *Allure*, August 31, 2021, https://www.allure.com/story/hair-loss-20s; G. Fabbrocini et al. "Female Pattern Hair Loss: A Clinical, Pathophysiologic, and Therapeutic Review," *International Journal of Women's Dermatology* 4, 4 (June 19, 2018): 203–211, https://doi.org/10.1016/j.ijwd.2018.05.001.

2. *Almost half of black women experience hair loss:* Crystal Ugochi Aguh, "Review of "Hair Loss in Black Women: Tips from an Expert," *Johns Hopkins Medicine*, https://www.hopkinsmedicine.org/health/wellness-and-prevention/hair-loss-in-black-women-tips-from-an-expert.

3. *CCCA can appear in a woman's twenties or thirties:* Sierra Leone Starks, "Why This Common Form of Hair Loss in Black Women Is Often Misdiagnosed," *Allure*, August 31, 2021, https://www.allure.com/story/central-centrifugal-cicatricial-alopecia.

Embracing Those in Our Community Who Have Alopecia & Alopecia Remedies

1. *Zinc supplements can help treat hair loss:* G. Fabbrocini, M. Cantelli, A. Masarà, M.C. Annunziata, C. Marasca, and S. Cacciapuoti, "Female Pattern Hair Loss: A Clinical, Pathophysiologic, and Therapeutic Review," *Int J Womens Dermatol* 4, 4 (June 19, 2018): 203–211. https://doi.org/10.1016/j.ijwd.2018.05.001; H. Park, C.W, Kim, S.S. Kim, and C.W. Park, "The Therapeutic Effect and the Changed Serum Zinc Level After Zinc Supplementation in Alopecia Areata Patients Who Had a Low Serum Zinc Level," *Annals of Dermatology* 2, 2 (2009): 142–146. https://doi.org/10.5021/ad.2009.21.2.142.

What Makes Fragrance Less Safe

1. *Fragrance can contain phthalates, which are linked to possible preterm birth and impaired underdevelopment in girls:* Roni

Rabin, "A Call for Action on Toxic Chemicals," *New York Times*, July 1, 2016, https://archive.nytimes.com/well.blogs.nytimes.com/2016/07/01/a-call-for-action-on-toxic-chemicals/?_r=0.

Biotin

1. https://health.clevelandclinic.org/is-biotin-as-good-as-advertised-for-your-hair-loss/.

36S Herbs to Know: Thyme, Basil, Ginger & Neem

1. *Thyme and a mix of essential oils can promote hair growth:* C. Hay, M. Jamieson, and A.D. Ormerod, "Randomized trial of aromatherapy. Successful treatment for alopecia areata," *Archives of Dermatology* 134, 11 (1998): 1349–1352. https://pubmed.ncbi.nlm.nih.gov/9828867/.